CW00546994

INVERKEITHING TO THORNTON JUNCTION

via Cowdenbeath including colliery branches

Dennis Lovett & Allan McLean

Front cover: LNER K4 class 2-6-0 no. 61994 The Great Marquess *passes the site of Cowdenbeath North Junction (where the former main line diverged northwards towards Perth) on 22nd April 2012. The train had split at Thornton Junction and was working the Fort William leg of the 'Great Britain V'. (W.Roberton)*

*Back cover, upper: Two class 100 diesel multiple units head out of Dunfermline Lower on 22nd October 1966 with a train for Stirling via Oakley. These services continued to run until October 1968. (*ColourRail.com*)*

Back cover, lower: Railway Clearing House map (edited), dated 1941. The route of the album is shown with a dotted line.

Readers of this book may be interested in the following societies:

North British Railway Study Group
www.nbrstudygroup.co.uk

Industrial Railway Society
www.irsociety.co.uk

Scottish Railway Preservation Society
Bo'ness & Kinneil Railway
www.srps.org.uk

Stephenson Locomotive Society
www.stephensonloco.org.uk

Published February 2023

ISBN 978 1 910356 76 0

Cover design and Photographic enhancement Deborah Esher
Production Cassandra Morgan

Published by
Middleton Press Ltd
Camelsdale Road
Haslemere
Surrey
GU27 3RJ
Tel: 01730 813169
Email: info@middletonpress.co.uk
www.middletonpress.co.uk

Printed and bound by CPI Group (UK) Ltd, Croydon, CR0 4YY

SECTIONS

CONTENTS

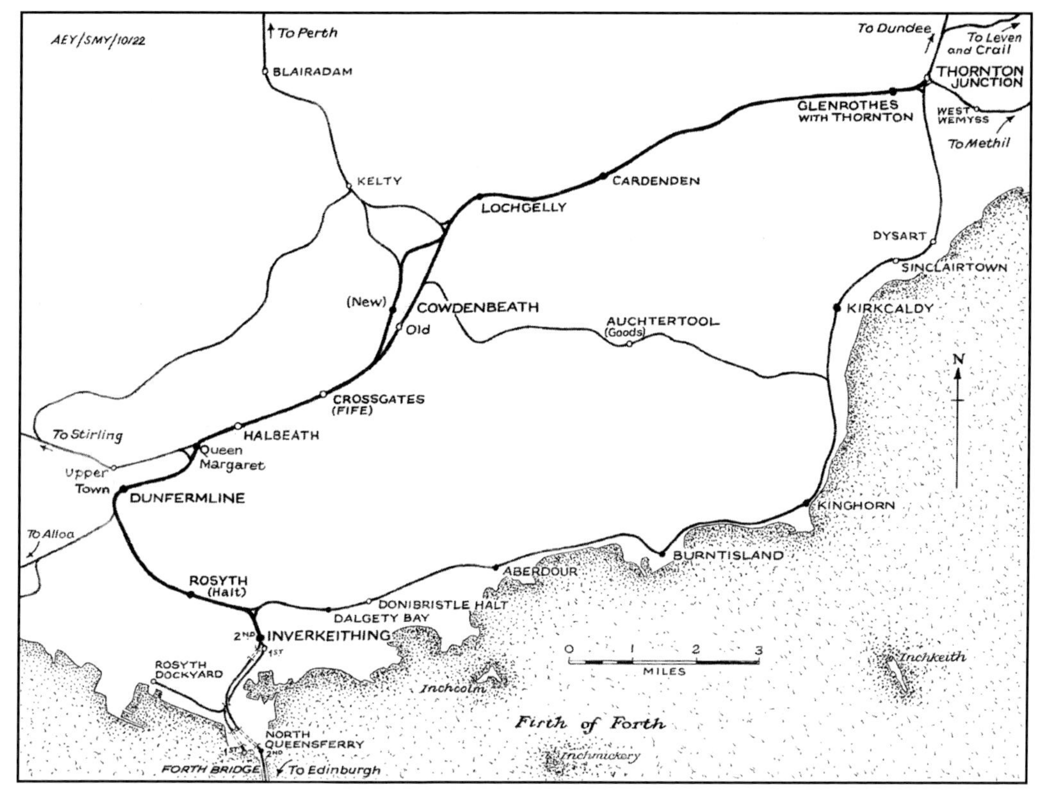

I. A map of the lines covered in this album are shown in solid black. (A.E.Young)

ACKNOWLEDGEMENTS

We are grateful for the assistance received from many of those mentioned in the photographic credits and to, A. Barrie, D.Bell (Assistant Curator National Mining Museum Scotland), J. M. Cameron, G. Croughton, R.R.Darsley, F.Fernandes (ScotRail), G. Gartside, C.M. Howard, E.Kidd, N. Langridge, A. McLean (National Railway Museum), E. McKenna, W.Roberton, D. and Dr S. Salter, A. Simpson, M. Stewart, J. Summers, J.P.Vickers, P.Westwater, M.Williams, D.Yellowlees, J.W.Yellowlees (ScotRail) and A.E.Young.

GEOGRAPHICAL SETTING

The Kingdom of Fife is a peninsula that lies between the Forth Estuary in the south and the Tay Estuary to the north.

The Firth of Forth was created by volcanic and glacial activity during the last ice age. The Forth separates Lothian in the south and Fife before flowing into the North Sea. Inverkeithing and its harbour are on the Forth estuary.

The area covered by this album was at the heart of the Fife coalfield, which spread from the border with Clackmannanshire in the west towards Methil on the coast. Pits covered in this album were located around Dunfermline, Cowdenbeath, Lochgelly and Thornton. Coal was extracted by both deep and open cast mining and, by the 1950s, the Fife field was the largest and most important in Scotland. No coal is mined today although some reminders as to its past importance remain in the former mining towns and villages.

Maps are derived from 25ins to 1 mile editions with north at the top unless otherwise stated.

HISTORICAL BACKGROUND

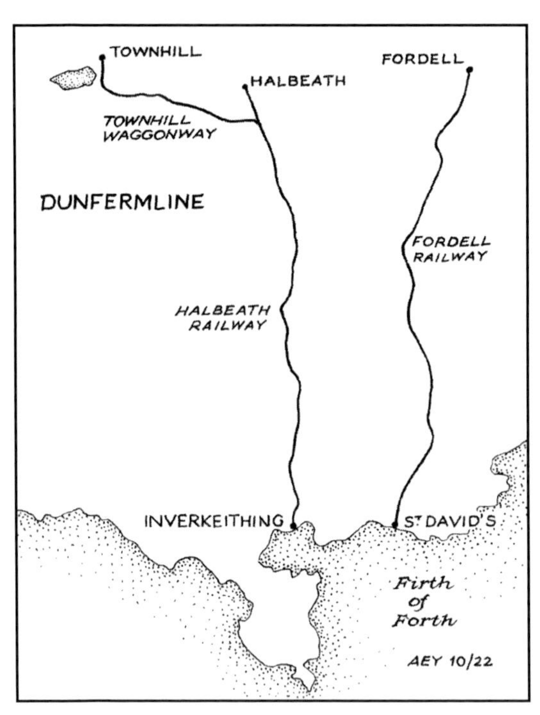

II. Early railways in Fife connecting coal pits to the Firth of Forth harbours. (A.E.Young)

The Kingdom of Fife, so named because Dunfermline was once home to the ancient Scottish Kings and the later Stuart Kings and Queens who hunted at Falkland. Dunfermline was Scotland's capital until 1437 when following the murder of James 1st, the Scottish Royal Family moved to the safety of Edinburgh Castle.

Coal had been mined in Fife from the 12th Century and it was coal that resulted in the first waggonways being developed to carry coal from the mines to the Forth Estuary. Three such lines were constructed two of which, the northern ends of the Fordell Railway and the Halbeath Railway, fall within the area of this album. They both took coal from the Dunfermline areas to the harbours at St. David's and Inverkeithing, respectively.

The Fordell Railway ran from the Fordell pit to the harbour at St. David's, a mile or so east of Inverkeithing. The owners, the Henderson family, initially transported coal by horses with panniers fitted either side. The harbour dates from around 1750 and, by the early 1770s, a wooden waggonway, with a track gauge of 4ft 4in, four miles long, had been built to take the coal down to the harbour. Later extensions increased the length of the line to just under 6 miles. To accommodate the growing traffic the harbour at St David's was enlarged in 1826 and 1832 respectively. Three inclines eased the gradients down to the harbour. Steam operation commenced in 1868 and access to some of the pits was shared with the main line railway resulting in dual gauge track being laid in places to accommodate wagons of both the 4ft 4in and standard gauge (4ft 8½in) lines. When the connecting line between Inverkeithing and Burntisland was being built in conjunction with the Forth Bridge, which opened in 1890, the new line had to bridge the Fordell line.

On nationalisation of the coal industry in 1947, the Fordell Railway became part of the National Coal Board Area 1. The final shipment of coal left St David's Harbour on 10th August 1946 after which the Southern section of the line was abandoned. The northern end of the line continued in use serving the various collieries until 1966.

The Halbeath Railway ran for 5 miles from the Crossgates area to the harbour at Inverkeithing. It opened in 1783 using wooden track built to 4ft 4in gauge. By 1811 iron rails were in use and in 1841 a branch to Townhill Colliery was opened, known as the Townhill waggonway. The opening of the branch from Thornton Junction to Dunfermline by the Edinburgh & Northern Railway resulted in a dispute with the Halbeath Railway which it required to cross on the level. After a lengthy dispute, the level crossing was finally approved, and the line reached Dunfermline in 1849.

The arrival of the Edinburgh & Northern saw connections made to the various collieries in the area and sounded the death knell of the Halbeath Railway with coal trains being sent to the larger harbour at Burntisland. It was eventually acquired by the North British Railway (NBR) and closed in 1871, the NBR failing to secure a buyer for what its shareholders considered to be a bad investment! The southern end of the line was used as the Inverkeithing Harbour branch that opened in 1877.

Edinburgh & Northern Railway

Authorised in 1845, the Edinburgh & Northern Railway linked Burntisland to both Perth and Dundee.

At Burntisland the Edinburgh & Northern built an impressive terminal station to connect with the ferries from Granton across the Firth of Forth, a rail link being provided between Canal Street in Edinburgh (adjacent to North Bridge later Waverley station) to Granton Harbour. From Burntisland a line to Ladybank was built north from Thornton Junction, which formed the junction for the lines to split to both Perth and Tayport where another ferry took passengers to Dundee.

Included in the Edinburgh & Northern Railway Act was the building of a line from Thornton to Dunfermline. Built with its eye on the expected levels of coal traffic that it could carry from the West Fife coalfield to the harbour at Burntisland. The line would serve the coal mines around Lochgelly and Cowdenbeath.

Opened as far as Crossgates in 1848, the line onwards to Dunfermline opened on 13th December 1849 following a dispute with the Halbeath Railway. It terminated at what would later become Dunfermline Upper station and formed an end to end connection with the Stirling & Dunfermline Railway, which had reached Dunfermline via Alloa.

Gradient Profile covering the section from Cowdenbeath to Thornton South Junction. (A.E.Young)

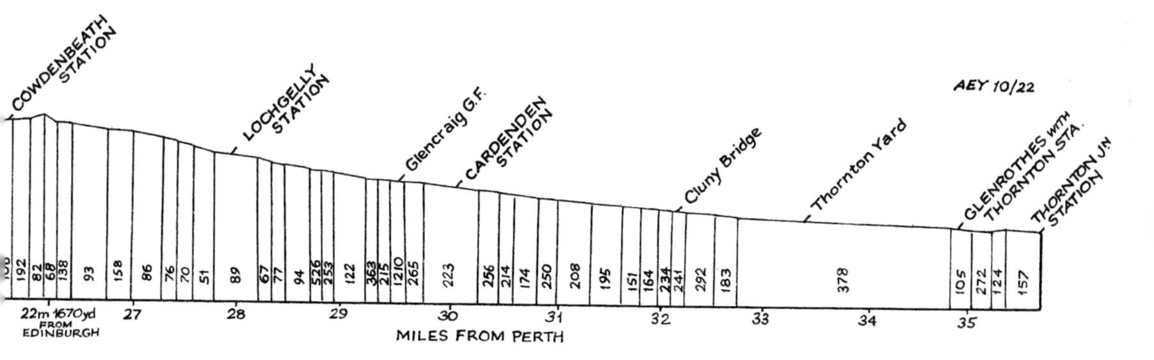

Dunfermline & Queensferry Railway

The first railway to serve Inverkeithing was the Dunfermline & Queensferry that connected Dunfermline to the ferry at North Queensferry. Opened on 1st April 1878, by which time the line had been taken over by the NBR, it served Inverkeithing. The opening of the Forth Bridge on 4th March 1890 had a dramatic effect on railways both north and south of the Forth Estuary and catapulted them to main line status. With it came a new station for Inverkeithing. Further details of this railway south of Inverkeithing can be found in our *Edinburgh to Inverkeithing* album.

Gradient Profile for the Inverkeithing to Cowdenbeath North section. (A.E.Young)

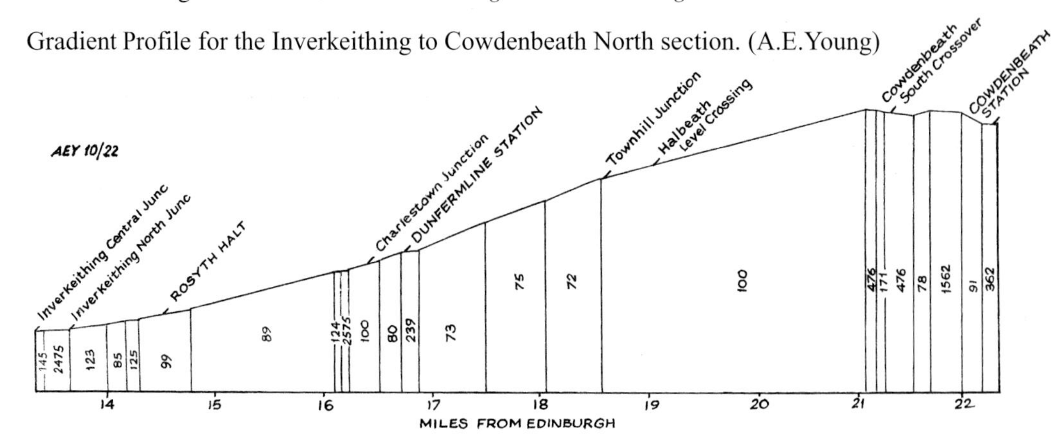

Perth Direct Railway

The final piece of the jigsaw was the building of the Perth Direct line, which, like the Inverkeithing to Burntisland line, was built in conjunction with the opening of the Forth Bridge in 1890. Branching off the original line south of Cowdenbeath it formed a loop back on to the original route at Lumphinnans Central Junction. At Cowdenbeath North Junction a junction was formed to take the line to Kelty and thence over Glenfarg to Perth.

EDINBURGH, DUNFERMLINE, THORNTON, ALLOA, and STIRLING.—North British.

Week Days only.

Miles.	Station	aft	mrn	mrn	mrn Thursdays only.	mrn	mrn	aft	mrn	mrn	aft	aft	mrn	aft	aft	aft	aft	mrn	aft				
	366 London (K.C.)..dep	7c45						1030					4 55					10 0					
	576 " (St. Pan.) "	mrn						9 10										9 15					
—	Edinburgh (Wav.)..dep.	5 28					7 55	8 25			1228		4 0					8 15					
1¼	Haymarket........ "	5 33					8 0	8 30			1233		4 6					8 21					
3½	Saughton.......... "																						
6¼	Turnhouse.[Queensfy"						8 9				1243		4 16										
9½	Dalmeny, for South "	5 47					8 17				1252		4 25					8 37					
11¾	North Queensferry. "	5 54					8 24				1259		4 32										
13½	Inverkeithing...... "	6 0					8 31				1 6		4 39					8 49					
16¾	Dunferm-line (Lower) arr.	6 8					8 41	8 55			1 14		4 47					8 57					
	(Lower) dep.	6 13						9 17			1 19		4 54					9 4					
19¼	" (Upper).. arr.	6 20						9 24			1 26		5 1					9 11					
—	846 Aberdeen .... dep.															1230			5 0				
—	846 Dundee (Tay B.) "			6 17		7 32			9 50			1 24				3 2			7 29				
—	Mls Thornton .....dep.			8 2		8 42			11 5			3 15				6 10			9 5				
—	5¼ Cardenden			8 15					1116			3 26				6 22			9 17				
—	7¾ Lochgelly.........			8 24					1125			3 33				6 28			9 23				
—	9½ Cowdenbeath (New)			8 32		9 3			1132			3 42				6 37			9 30				
—	11½ Crossgates........			8 37								3 51				6 46			9 39				
—	13 Halbeath [851, 872			8 39																			
—	15¼ Dunferm- (L.).. arr.					9 12			1141	1145													
	line (Up.) "			8 48						1152		4 0				6 55			9 48				
—	Dunfermline (Up)..dep.	6 25						9 27		1155	1 31		5 4					9 14					
23¾	Oakley..............	6 34						9 36		12 5	1 41		5 12					9 23					
25½	East Grange..........	6 39						9 41		1210	1 46		5 17					9 28					
27½	Bogside..............	6 45						9 47		1216			5 22										
29¾	Forest Mill...........	6 52						9 54		1223													
30¾	Clackmannan Road.....																						
33	Alloa 849 853, 872 arr.	7 0						10 1		1229	1 58		5 30					9 42					
	dep.	7 5	8 2		9 25			10 5		1250	2 2		5 33	5 50	6 30		7 30	9 45					
35	Cambus.*.............	7 11	8 7		9 30			1011		1256	2 7			5 55	6 35		7 35	9 51					
38½	Causewayhead †.......																						
39¾	Stirling 851, 902..arr.	7 20	8 16		9 39			1020		1 5	2 16		5 44	6 4	6 44		7 44	10 0					

Although the Perth line closed in 1970, today's trains continue to use the line through Cowdenbeath (New), which now is the only route between Dunfermline and Thornton Junction and is used by ScotRail's local trains. The Perth Direct Line will be the subject of a future album.

PASSENGER SERVICES

The opening of the Forth Bridge in 1890 revolutionised rail services in this area with the building of a new line and station at Inverkeithing elevating it to main line status. Prior to that the line between Dunfermline and North Queensferry provided a link to the ferry service across the Firth of Forth where another line from South Queensferry to Edinburgh allowed passengers to reach the capital city. Full coverage of both lines can be found in our *Edinburgh to Inverkeithing* album.

Following the publication of *The Reshaping of British Railways* in 1963, many branch lines closed and many stations on existing lines closed. The route between Inverkeithing and Cowdenbeath remained a main line until closure of the Perth direct line in 1970. Local DMU services continued to serve Dunfermline Lower and Cowdenbeath with some services continuing during peak hours only to serve Lochgelly and Cardenden.

Coal remained an important commodity and provided much needed traffic to and from the yard at Thornton which, beyond Cardenden, was restricted to one passenger train a day in only one direction.

On 15th May 1989 the line beyond Cardenden to Thornton Junction reopened for passenger trains, although the station at Thornton Junction had closed with the Leven line 20 years earlier. Trains used the west to south junction to return to Edinburgh Waverley via Burntisland and Inverkeithing. These became known as the Fife Circle services, with trains also running in the opposite direction.

In May 2022, the timetables for Fife services were completely revised following a fall in passenger numbers post the Covid 19 Pandemic. The line between Inverkeithing and Glenrothes with Thornton currently has an hourly all stations service and an hourly service terminating at Cowdenbeath. All trains are worked by ScotRail diesel multiple units, although electrification is proposed for part of the route initially. This will require new battery-electric trains to be procured.

					Z		SX					Z						D Z				SX			
Aberdeen	229 d			14 40							15 35						16 30				17 12			
Stonehaven	229 d			15 00							15 55						16 51				17 32			
Montrose	229 d			15 26							16 21						17 17							
Arbroath	229 d		15 21	15 42					16 16		16 37					17 16	17 33							
Carnoustie	229 d		15 29						16 24							17 24								
Golf Street Halt	229 d		15 32						16 27							17 27								
Barry Links	229 d								16 30															
Monifieth	229 d		15 38						16 35							17 33								
Balmossie Halt	229 d		15 41						16 38							17 36								
Broughty Ferry	229 d		15 45						16 42							17 40								
Dundee	a		15 53	16 04					16 50		16 59					17 48	17 56							
	d			16 06			16 20				17 01		17 20				18 00	18 20						
Leuchars	d						16 34						17 34				18 14	18 34						
Cupar	d						16 43						17 43					18 43						
Springfield	d						16 48						17 48					18 48						
Perth	229 d																							
Ladybank	d						16 53						17 53					18 53						
Markinch for Glenrothes	d						17 03						18 03					19 03						
Kirkcaldy	d			16 46		16 52	17 12					17 50	18 12				18 42	19 12				19 50		
Kinghorn	d					16 57	17 18						18 18					19 18						
Burntisland	d					17 02	17 22						18 22					19 22						
Aberdour	d					17 08	17 28						18 28					19 28						
Cardenden	d													18 11										
Lochgelly	d													18 16										
Cowdenbeath	d	16 25						17 22						18 22					19 22					
Dunfermline	d	16 34						17 31						18 31					19 31					
Rosyth Halt	d	16 38						17 35						18 35					19 35					
Inverkeithing	d	16 42		17 04		17 15	17 35	17 39				18 08	18 35	18 39			19 01	19 35	19 39			20 08		
North Queensferry	d	16 47				17 20		17 44						18 44					19 44					
Dalmeny	d	16 51						17 48						18 48					19 48					
Haymarket	65, 225, 228 a	17 01		17 24		17 32	17 52	17 58				18 23	18 52	18 58			19 20	19 52	19 58			20 23		
228 Glasgow Queen Street	229 a	18 19		18 19		18 49	18 49	19 19			18g36	19 19	19 47	20 19			20 19	20 47	21 19			21 19		
Edinburgh	65. 225. 228 a	17 05		17 27		17 35	17 56	18 02				18 26	18 56	19 02			19 23	19 56	20 02			20 26		

← 1917 timetable for the Up direction showing services via Cowdenbeath (New).

↑ 1980 Up timetable showing the spartan peak hours-only service provision for Cardenden and Lochgelly. Thornton Junction had closed in 1969 and no longer appeared in the timetable.

1. Inverkeithing to Cowdenbeath South Junction via Dunfermline

INVERKEITHING

III. This station is the second to serve the town as seen in this 1925 map. The first station was opened on 1st November 1877 by the Dunfermline & Queensferry Railway following the opening of the line from Dunfermline to the terminus at North Queensferry Pier. It consisted of a single platform and was replaced due to the opening of the Forth Bridge on 4th March 1890 by a new station, situated some 12 chains north of the original as the new double track main line from the bridge by-passed the original station. The original station was officially closed on 2nd June 1890.

The current station received a new main building on the down platform, which was opened in 1985. Inverkeithing is served by the Aberdeen portion of the Caledonian Sleeper, ScotRail and London North Eastern Railway (LNER). CrossCountry trains pass through but no longer stop at any stations in Fife. The goods yard to the south of the station closed on 11th September 1967. Over the years, facilities north of the station were enlarged to handle interchange traffic with the Dockyard and for wagonload traffic for the surrounding area. It was later used for loading locally mined opencast coal, ballast from Cruiks Quarry and vehicles for scrap at RM Supplies yard (formerly T.W.Ward). The remaining sidings remain in use for civil engineer's trains and receive regular visits from track machines and other rail related equipment.

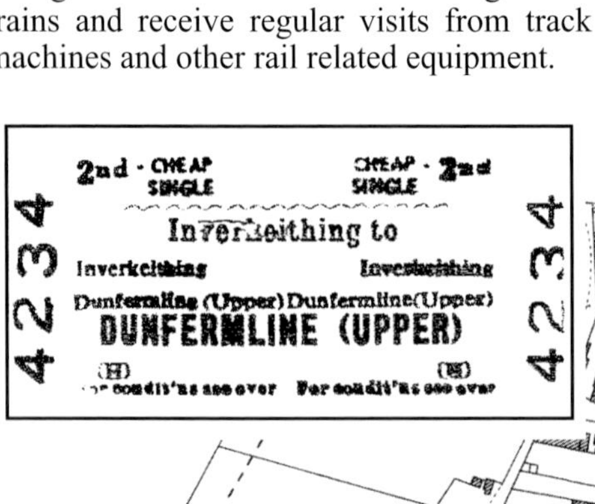

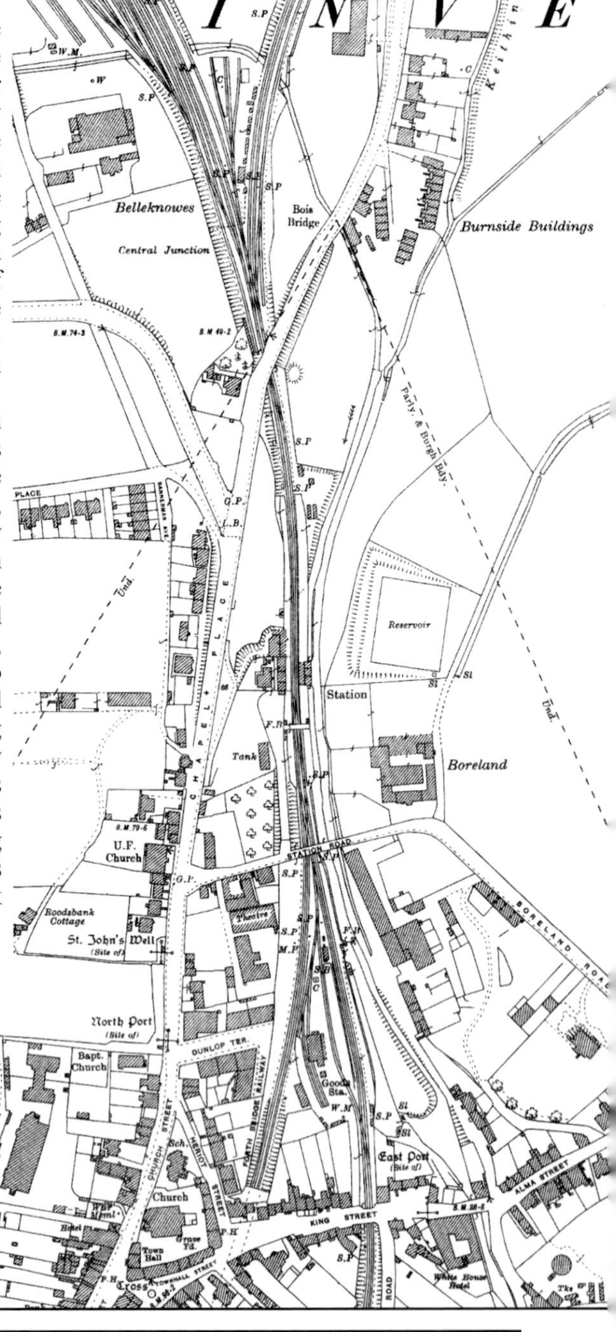

The section of line from North Queensferry Pier to Inverkeithing is covered in our *Edinburgh to Inverkeithing* album.

1. The photographer is standing on the Boreland Road bridge in August 1965 looking north. The junction signal is set for the main line to Edinburgh, the other serving the former North Queensferry branch. (*ColourRail.com*)

2. J37 class 0-6-0 no. 64620 heads north with a freight train on 7th April 1966. (T.Owen/*ColourRail.com*)

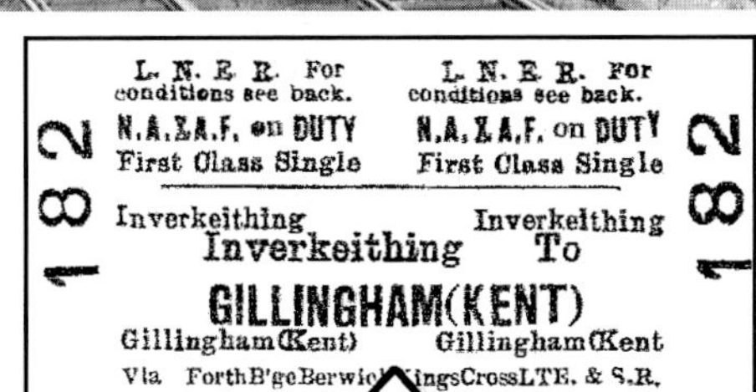

182

L. N. E. R. For conditions see back.
N.A.&A.F. on DUTY
First Class Single
Inverkeithing
Gillingham(Kent)

L. N. E. R. For conditions see back.
N.A.&A.F. on DUTY
First Class Single
Inverkeithing
Gillingham(Kent

182

Inverkeithing To
GILLINGHAM(KENT)
Via ForthB'geBerwickKingsCrossLTE. & S.R.

3. Class 47 no. 47702 departs with the 17.42 from Edinburgh Waverley to Kirkcaldy on 10th August 1983 with the Forth Bridge providing an impressive background. (G.W.Morrison)

4. Class 170 no. 170427 calls with a Fife Circle service for Glenrothes with Thornton on 19th July 2019. (D.A.Lovett)

Inverkeithing Central Junction

5. Just beyond the station lies Inverkeithing Central Junction where the 1890 lines, built as part of the Forth Bridge scheme, turn east to join up with the original Edinburgh & Northern line at Burntisland and turn west to Thornton Junction via Cowdenbeath. Prior to the opening of the bridge, Burntisland had previously been the interchange point between the goods and passenger ferries from Granton and the trains, Burntisland then being a terminus station.

The line heading towards the west was the original line of the Dunfermline & Queensferry Railway, which, until 1890, terminated at Dunfermline Comely Park. The line was rebuilt to double track as part of the new direct line to Perth, which also formed part of the Forth Bridge scheme. This is illustrated at the top of map III, on the previous page.

Inverkeithing lies in a dip and in steam days the gradients in all three directions constituted a challenge to those on the footplate.

The bi-directional signals and points that form the Central Junction are viewed from the up platform on 26th June 2011. The left-hand route is the one we are taking. The former loco yard was located in the 'V' of the junction, now covered by trees in the centre of the picture. (D.A.Lovett)

6. Coal dominates this album and is typified by two Merry Go Round (MGR) trains running to and from the pits and Longannet power station on Sunday 5th March 1972. Longannet was located on the north bank of the Firth of Forth, near Kincardine, on the line between Alloa and Charlestown Junction. A train of empties heads back to the pit for reloading whilst a class 20, with a full train, passes Inverkeithing Central Junction box and heads towards Inverkeithing station. The line branching off to the right forms part of the main line via Burntisland and Kirkcaldy. (J.M.Summers)

Inverkeithing Locomotive Yard

In British Railways (BR) days the locomotive yard here was classified as a sub shed of 62C Dunfermline. No shed building was ever provided, facilities were basic with just a coaling stage, water column and an inspection pit. A facility was provided from 1st November 1877 most likely in the goods yard south of the station. The facility shown here opened post World War I and appeared first on 1925 maps, closing on 31st December 1966. A notable feature was that banking engines for trains up to the Forth Bridge ran tender-first, in order to spare the crews the smoke from their own engines in the tunnels.

7. The modest facilities here benefitted from a crane to load coal from the wagons into locomotive tenders using the tubs provided when visited on 2nd September 1959. (W.T.Stubbs/R.S.Carpenter)

Inverkeithing North Junction

➚ IV. Located at the north end of the triangle, North Junction allows trains from the Burntisland route to access the Dunfermline line using the north chord and vice-versa, a key route in later years for the MGR coal trains from the east to Longannet. This was the location in 1915.

Inverkeithing Brick & Tile Works

➔ V. The Rosyth Brick & Tile Company was formed in 1915 and, by the following year, was producing 10,000 bricks a day using clay from the adjacent pit. At its peak, production could reach some 60,000 bricks per day. The establishment of a prisoner-of-war camp in 1917 saw some 72 German POW's providing labour on the site. Many of the red bricks were destined for the Royal Navy Dockyard at Rosyth. After the war, production continued until the General Strike in 1926 which forced its closure and it never reopened once the strike had finished. The site was offered for sale in 1928 and attempts were made to recommence production in 1938 but failed to materialise. The kilns and their chimneys were subsequently demolished and the site cleared by 1948. This map is dated 1927.

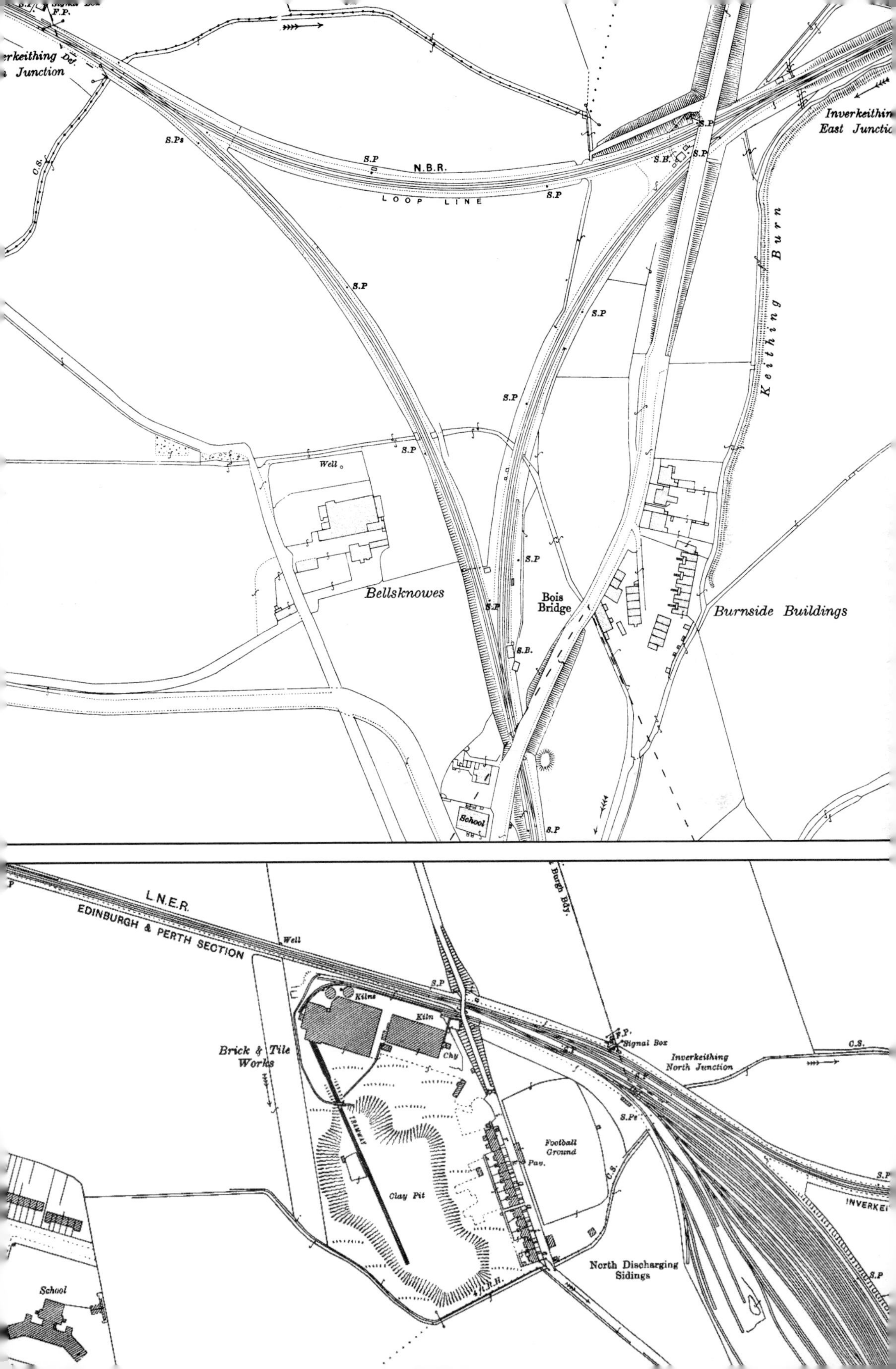

Inverkeithing Def.
Junction
F.P.
O.S.
S.Ps
S.P
N.B.R.
LOOP LINE
S.B.
Inverkeithing
East Junction
Keithing Burn
Well
Bellsknowes
Bois
Bridge
S.B.
Burnside Buildings
School
L.N.E.R.
EDINBURGH & PERTH SECTION
Well
Kilns
Kiln
Chy
Brick & Tile
Works
Burgh Bdy.
Signal Box
Inverkeithing
North Junction
C.S.
TRAMWAY
Clay Pit
Football
Ground
Pav.
S.Ps
North Discharging
Sidings
INVERKEI
School

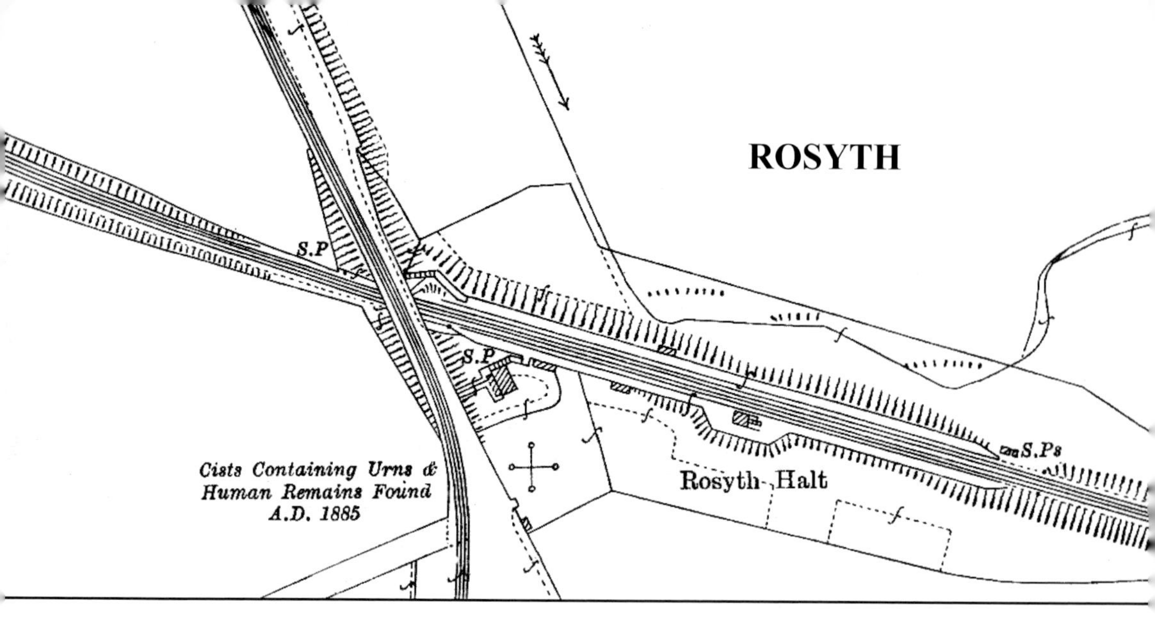

VI. This station opened on 1st January 1918 as Rosyth Halt to serve the dockyard which lay two miles to the south of the station. This 1926 map shows how isolated it was at that time, but, today, there is considerable development around the station. It was renamed Rosyth on 16th May 1983 and is served by ScotRail.

8. Looking north in around 1917. The signal box is seen, with the elevated booking office in the distance. (Lens of Sutton Association)

9. Looking towards Dunfermline on 12th April 1954. It would be another 29 years before 'Halt' was dropped from the name-boards. (R.W.Lynn coll.)

10. The booking office was still in position on 20th April 1985 but has subsequently been demolished and the station rebuilt to provide ramped access to both platforms. (A.E.Young)

11. Passengers wait to join class 158 no. 158870, which forms the 14.06 service south to Edinburgh Waverley on 1st August 2011. (D.A.Lovett)

Charlestown Junction

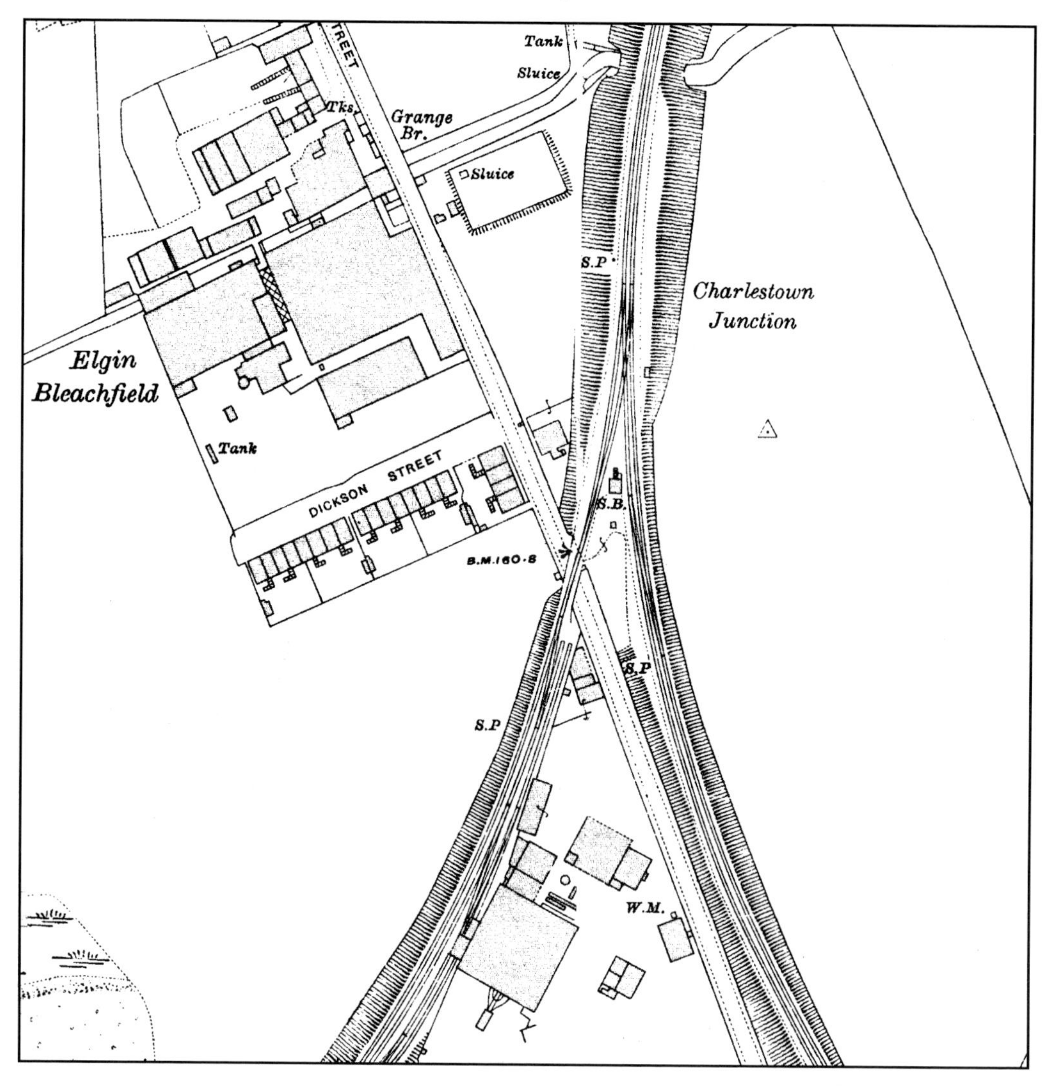

VII. The line from Stirling via Alloa and Kincardine joins here as seen on this 1915 map. It formed a junction with the line from Dunfermline to Charlestown at Elbowend Junction from 1903.

The line between Alloa and Kincardine opened in 1893 and from Kincardine to Dunfermline in 1903. Due to disappointing passenger numbers the line closed to passengers in 1930. After World War II the central section was used for wagon storage, with the eastern section kept in use to serve Valleyfield Colliery. The line was re-opened throughout for coal trains to serve from east or west Longannet Power Station, construction of which started in 1965 and took five years before it was commissioned in 1970. Following closure of the adjacent mine complex, which had supplemented the coal trains from east Fife and Ayrshire pits, coal had been imported via Hunterston in Ayrshire and transported by rail.

In 1985 the through route was taken out of use and mothballed between Longannet and Alloa West Junction. The mothballed section from Alloa to Longannet was reopened in 2008 to freight traffic following the rebuilding of the Stirling to Alloa line and the reinstatement of passenger services on 19th May 2008. The coal from the west could now run via the simpler route via Stirling and thus yield capacity on the Forth Bridge for increased passenger services.

The Charlestown branch, which the line from Alloa met at Elbowend Junction, had preceded it, having opened on 1st September 1894. It lost its passenger service on 1st November 1926, before closing to goods on 24th February 1964. Part of the line remained open to serve Royal Naval Armament Depot Crombie until December 1990.

With the direct line between Dunfermline and Stirling via Alloa having been closed to passenger traffic from 7th October 1968 and goods services following the closure of Oakley Colliery in 1984, the secondary line via Kincardine and Longannet became the only route between these two centres. The end of the power station traffic meant the section between Alloa and Dunfermline was again mothballed, but saw occasional railtours. At the time of writing, it is in use for regular trains of ballast enroute to the new Levenmouth branch and is itself the subject of a reopening campaign. There are also plans to open a new rolling stock construction facility on the site of Kincardine Power Station by Spanish manufacturer, Talgo, but its construction is dependent on the company securing new train building contracts in the UK.

12. John Cameron's LNER A4 class 4-6-2 no. 60009 *Union of South Africa* has long been associated with Fife since the mid-1960s when he purchased it and put it into use initially on the Lochty Private Railway. It is seen here heading for Dunfermline off the Alloa line on 14th August 1986 past the closed Charlestown Junction signal box, which was decommissioned on 7th December 1980 when control of the area was taken over by Edinburgh Signalling Centre. The young trainspotter was not known to the photographer. (W.Roberton)

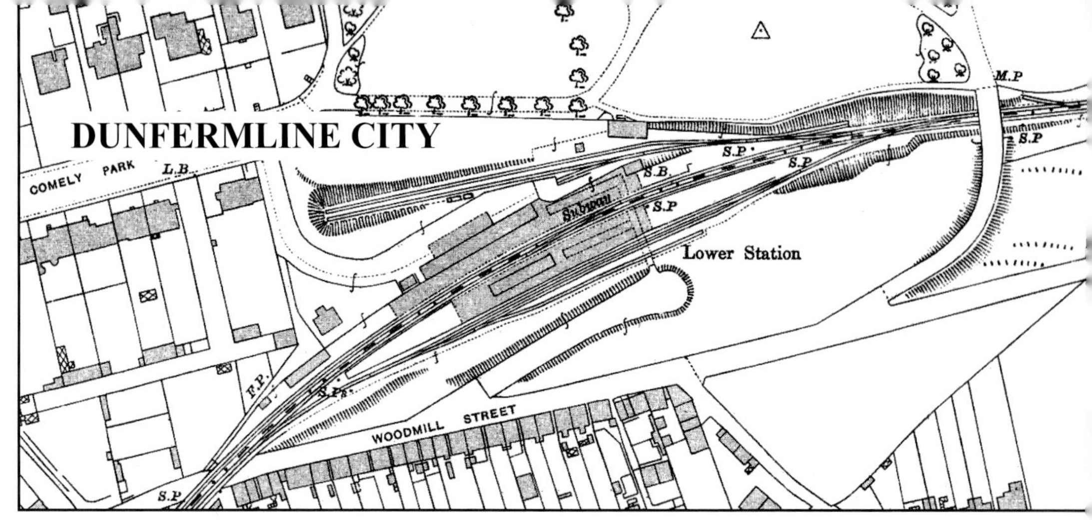

VIII. Opened on 1st November 1877 as Dunfermline Comely Bank, this station originally served as the terminus of the line from the pier at North Queensferry, which connected with the ferry service on the Queensferry crossing of the Firth of Forth.

Following the building of new routes in conjunction with the opening of the Forth Bridge, the station was rebuilt and renamed Dunfermline Lower on 26th October 1889. The town's other station was known as Dunfermline Upper and lay on the direct line from Stirling, which joined the line to Thornton at Townhill Junction. With the closure of Dunfermline Upper in 1969, the Lower station became plain Dunfermline. However, on 11th May 1987 it again appeared as Dunfermline Lower in timetables, reverting to Dunfermline a year later. With the opening of the additional station of Queen Margaret further north, Dunfermline became Dunfermline Town on 26th January 2000. It is served by ScotRail trains. The CCTV centre for the east of Scotland is located in the refurbished station building.

In 1960 the town's population was 46,270. In 2021 it was home to 50,380 giving it the largest population in Fife. Dunfermline was awarded city status in May 2022 as part of Her Majesty Queen Elizabeth II's Platinum Jubilee Celebrations, which took place just a few weeks before her passing. Following an official ceremony on 3rd October 2022, attended by King Charles III and the Queen Consort, it was revealed that the station would be renamed Dunfermline City.

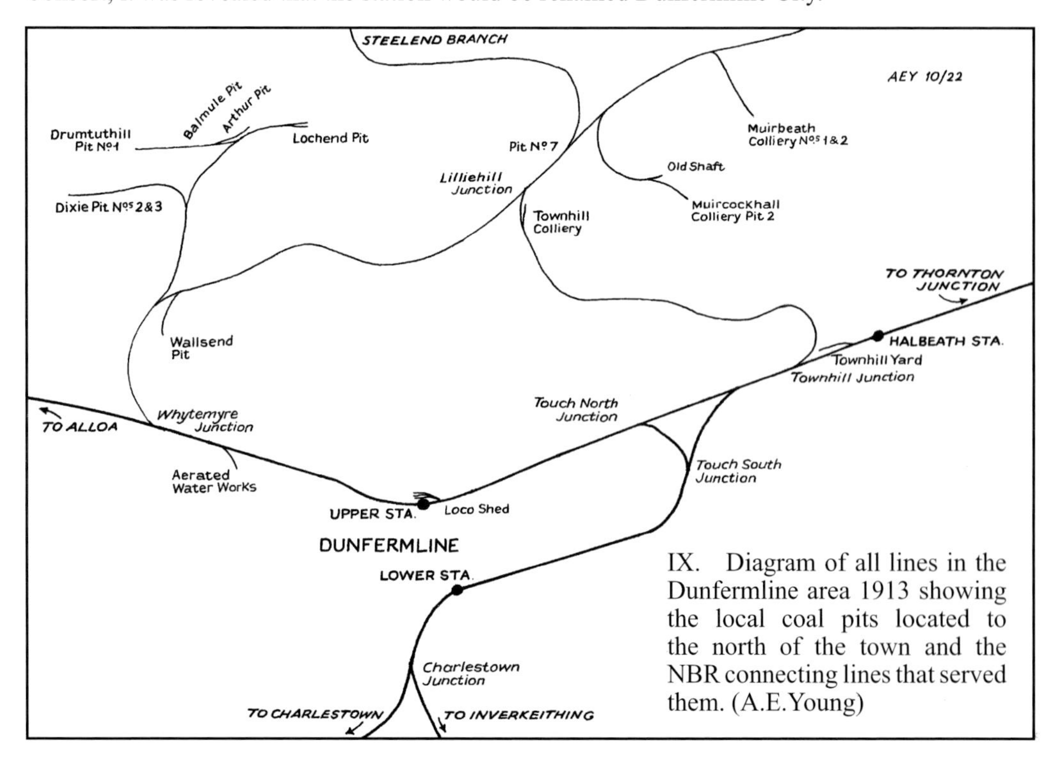

IX. Diagram of all lines in the Dunfermline area 1913 showing the local coal pits located to the north of the town and the NBR connecting lines that served them. (A.E.Young)

13. Peppercorn class A2 4-6-2 no. 60525 *A.H. Peppercorn* is near Dunfermline on 1st August 1953, heading an express to Edinburgh Waverley. It is taking the curves out of the station past the Prize Length sign awarded for outstanding permanent way work. (B.E.Morrison)

➔ Extract from *Bradshaws Guide 1866*, reprinted by Middleton Press, 2010.

DUNFERMLINE.

A telegraph station.
HOTELS.—Royal; Commercial.
MARKET DAY.—Tuesday.
FAIRS.—Third Tuesdays in January, February March, April, June, July, September, October, and November.

This is a large burgh town, in the county of Fife with a population of 13,506, who are engaged in the diaper, damask, and fine linen manufactures, and contains three Churches, seven Chapels, Town House, in which is a shirt without seam, woven by Inglis; Guildry, with a spire 132 feet high; Mechanics' Institute School of Design, libraries, market, mills, breweries, gas works, soap, tobacco, and candle factories. Bridge over a glen, built by Chalmers of Pittencrief. *St. Leonard's Hospital.* The church was rebuilt in 1820, and has a fine view over fourteen counties, from Ben Lomond to Loutra Hill; the nave of the old one still remains, in which lie buried Malcolm Canmore and his queen Margaret, whose shrine, in ruins, is shown. The bones of "The Bruce" were reburied under the pulpit in 1818. There are ruins of the Abbey and part of the wall of the palace which James the First's queen built, where Charles I. was born, and at which place he signed the covenant. Her bed is at Broomhall, and her cupboard at Pittencrief. It is built on an eminence, and has an irregular appearance, from its having been erected at various periods of time. The great object of attraction is its Abbey, part of which is now used as a Parish Church; the rest is in ruins, and convey but a faint picture of the former magnificence of the edifice.

Dunfermline has long been celebrated for different branches of weaving, but particularly that of table linen, which is said to be conducted more extensively here than in any other part of the United Kingdom.

042 N. B. R. 042
DUNFERMLINE
Lower Station To Lower Station
BLAIRADAM
Blairadam Blairadam
Via Kelty
1/8 1st CLASS 1st 1/8
Issued subject to the Bye-Laws and Regulations of the N.B.R. Company, and to the Conditions stated in their Public Time Tables. NOT TRANSFERABLE.

14. Naval Ratings head towards the station around 1914 at the start of World War I. (Lens of Sutton Association)

15. A local service to Edinburgh Waverley awaits departure from Dunfermline Lower on 1st August 1953, headed by Gresley V3 class 2-6-2T no. 67672, which was a Dunfermline (62C) allocated locomotive. (B.E.Morrison)

16. B1 class 4-6-0 no. 61076 and Black 5 no. 45433 pause at Dunfermline Lower with a heavy train on 20th April 1963 heading for Perth. (W.S.Sellar)

17. Class 20 Bo-Bo locomotives nos 20216 and 20218 pass with MGR empties destined for refilling at one of Fife's remaining collieries on 11th May 1977. (T.Heavyside)

18. The down platform, seen here on 10th August 1978, still retains the old Scottish Region signs and has plenty of trolleys ready for incoming parcels and postal traffic which had been concentrated on this station. (A.E.Young)

19. Dunfermline City houses ScotRail's CCTV monitoring centre for the east of Scotland in the main station building. It is seen here during a press visit on 23rd June 2005. (D.A.Lovett)

Dunfermline Pittencrief Park

20. A reminder of Fife's rich coal mining history can be found in Pittencrief Park, Dunfermline. Andrew Barclay 0-4-0ST Works no. 1996 built in 1934. It carries the livery of The Fife Coal Company although it never worked in the Kingdom having spent its time in East Lothian. It later worked at Bilston Glen south of Edinburgh. After many years in the park, it was restored by The Shed 47 Railway Restoration Group at the Scottish Vintage Bus Museum in Lathalmond. Pittencrief Park is a 15 minute walk from the station. (D.A.Lovett)

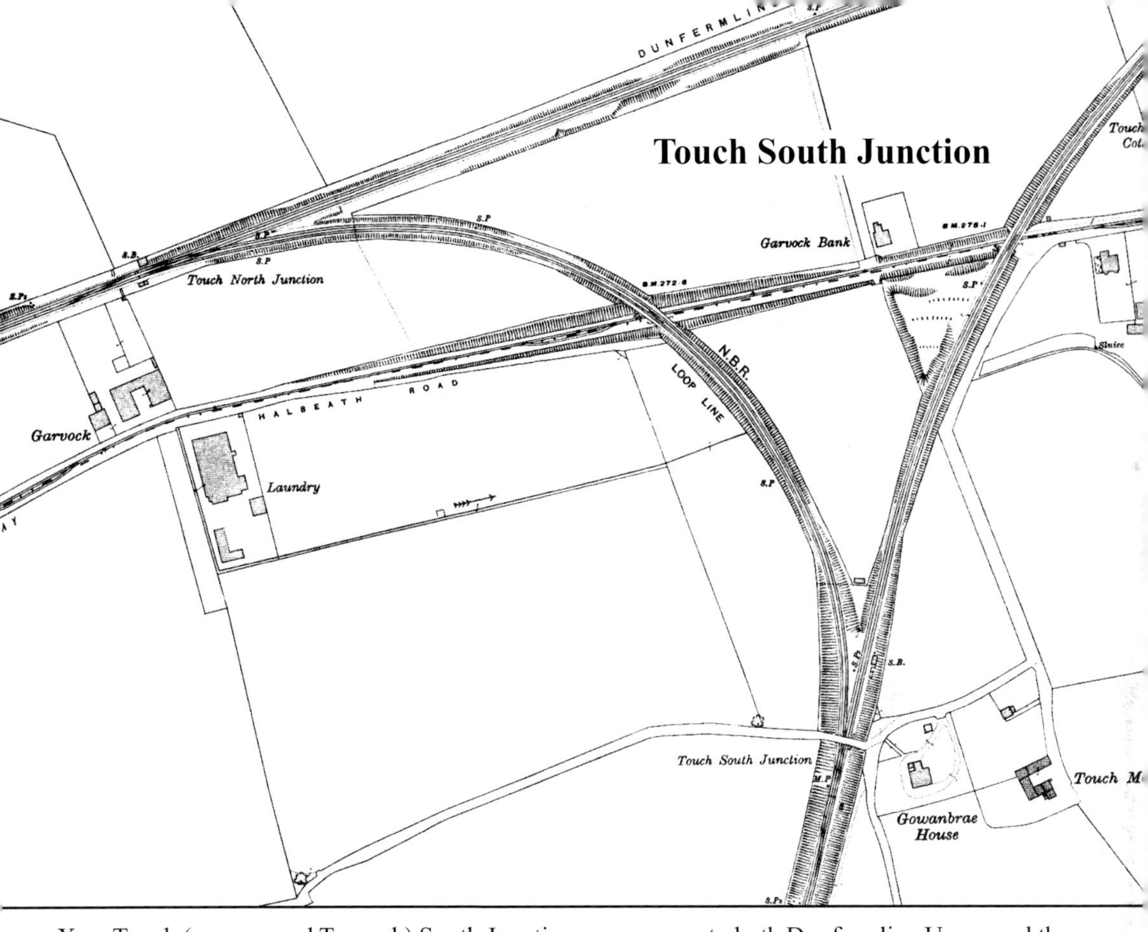

X. Touch (pronounced Too-och) South Junction gave access to both Dunfermline Upper and the various pits to the north of the town. Trams of the Dunfermline District Tramways ran along the Halbeath Road to Lochgelly. The 3ft 6in gauge tram system opened in 1909 and closed on 4th July 1937. It is seen running through the centre of the map, which dates from 1913.

21. The boarded-up signal box at Touch South Junction is seen here on 9th April 1971. The box had closed just a few months before, on 1st November 1970. (W.S.Sellar)

22. With the original line from Thornton Junction to Dunfermline (Upper) looking somewhat neglected, this view looks back towards Dunfermline with the floodlights of Dunfermline Athletic Football Club in the background. The line ran behind the ground. The vacated space now provides additional car parking on match days, the line having been lifted in 1986. (W.Roberton)

23. Looking in the opposite direction, this is the site of Touch South Junction on 11th December 2008 with class 158 no. 158725 heading towards Cowdenbeath. The line to Dunfermline Upper arrived from the left, the junction site being passed by the unit. After closure of the line from Dunfermline Upper, the Halbeath Road bridge was removed but the dip that allowed trams to pass underneath remains to this day. The unit is about to cross the remaining Halbeath Road bridge. (W.Roberton)

DUNFERMLINE QUEEN MARGARET

XI. This map shows the location of Dunfermline Queen Margaret and its proximity to the hospital with the same name. The station is built on the site of the former Townhill Junction.

Opened on 26th January 2000 it serves the east side of Dunfermline and the nearby Queen Margaret Hospital. The station consists of two platforms, shelters and a large footbridge, which meets full disability requirements. It has a large car park but no station building or other facilities.

The station is built on the site of the former Townhill Junction on the eastern, and only remaining, leg of a triangle formerly controlled by Touch North, Touch South and Townhill Junctions. The other legs were removed in 1970 and 1986.

The line from Townhill Junction to Touch North provided the original route from Thornton Junction into Dunfermline reaching the first station in the city, later known as Dunfermline Upper. Dunfermline Queen Margaret is served by ScotRail. (A.E.Young)

24. Looking east towards Cowdenbeath on 1st August 2011, this photograph shows the shelters and the footbridge accessed by the ramp or by steps. (D.A.Lovett)

Off-Peak Day Return Outward

Valid for one journey
from Dunfermline Queen Margaret
to Glenrothes

Date of travel
03-JUN-22

See restrictions nre.co.uk/H1
Adult Standard Class

Refundable and exchangeable for a fee

£6.10X 76888-4850-3914-21-05-00

1105:030622A

25. Class 158 no. 158719 calls at platform 1 with a service for Edinburgh Waverley, via Dunfermline, on 1st August 2011. (D.A.Lovett)

Townhill Junction and Sidings

XII. Townhill Yard was in place by 1895 to serve the trip trains for the various collieries around Dunfermline and is shown here in this 1913 map. The line heading off to the top served a number of pits to the north of Dunfermline and also provided an alternative route back to Dunfermline Upper.

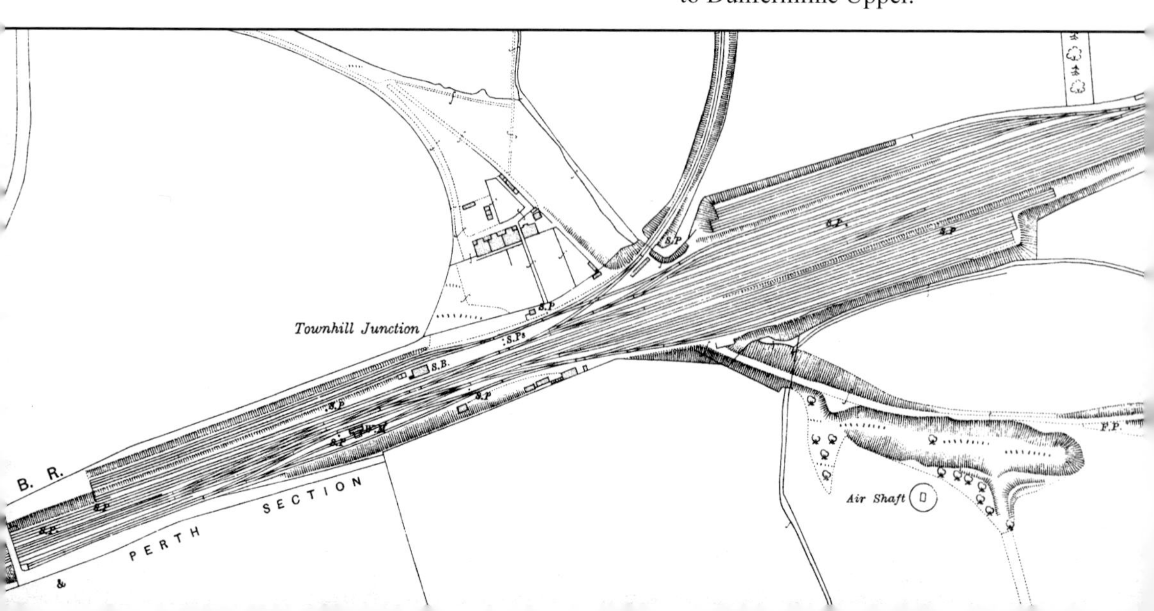

26. Class 56 no. 56061 is running round its train of empty MGR wagons from Longannet Power Station ready to return them to Hunterston for reloading with imported coal. We are looking towards Halbeath level crossing on 10th July 1998. (W.Roberton)

Townhill Wagon Works & Diesel Depot

27. 16 ton mineral wagons await attention outside the Wagon Repair works in 1974. The diesel depot is on the far side. (W.Roberton)

XIII. This 1961 map shows the British Railways wagon works that opened here after nationalisation in 1948 using rented premises. These were converted for railway use and located adjacent to the former Halbeath station, which is served by the road that crosses the line by a level crossing. Six steam locomotives were scrapped here in 1962. 157 staff were employed on site on 1st March 1967.

In March 1982, Townhill wagon shops produced a tunnel inspection vehicle for the Scottish Region's Chief Civil Engineer. Using the superstructure of a former unbraked vehicle, with extensions, the wagon used as a base was a BDV. The vehicle is coded YZV, with a number D8922925.

The wagon works closed on 24th January 1983. Part of the wagon works became the area's diesel depot following closure of the steam shed at Dunfermline Upper on 8th September 1969 as 62C.

The new depot opened on 5th October 1969 and was given the code 62C with effect from 1st July 1970. It carried the code DT (Dunfermline Townhill) from 5th May 1973.

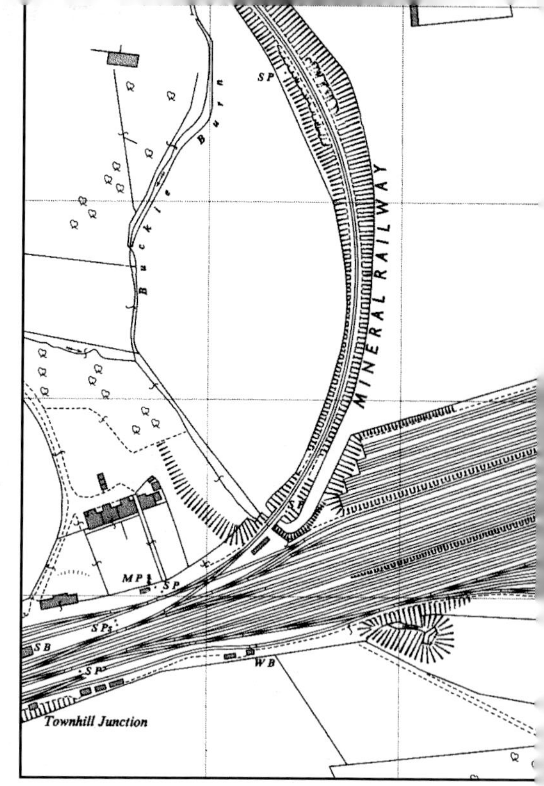

28. Seen here in 1983, the former wagon repair works and diesel depot await their fate. Closed in March of that year, the diesel depot was replaced by the 1984-built shed at Thornton Junction, but Townhill continued to be used to store withdrawn locomotives until December 1984. Works and depot were subsequently demolished. (W.Roberton)

➔ 29. Stored in a secure environment inside Townhill are class 20s nos 20007, 20108, 20040 and 20013 on 16th June 1983. (G.W.Morrison)

➘ 30. Class 08 diesel shunters, nos 08341 and 08452, are inside Townhill TMD on 11th September 1984. (P.M.Dunkley/*ColourRail.com*)

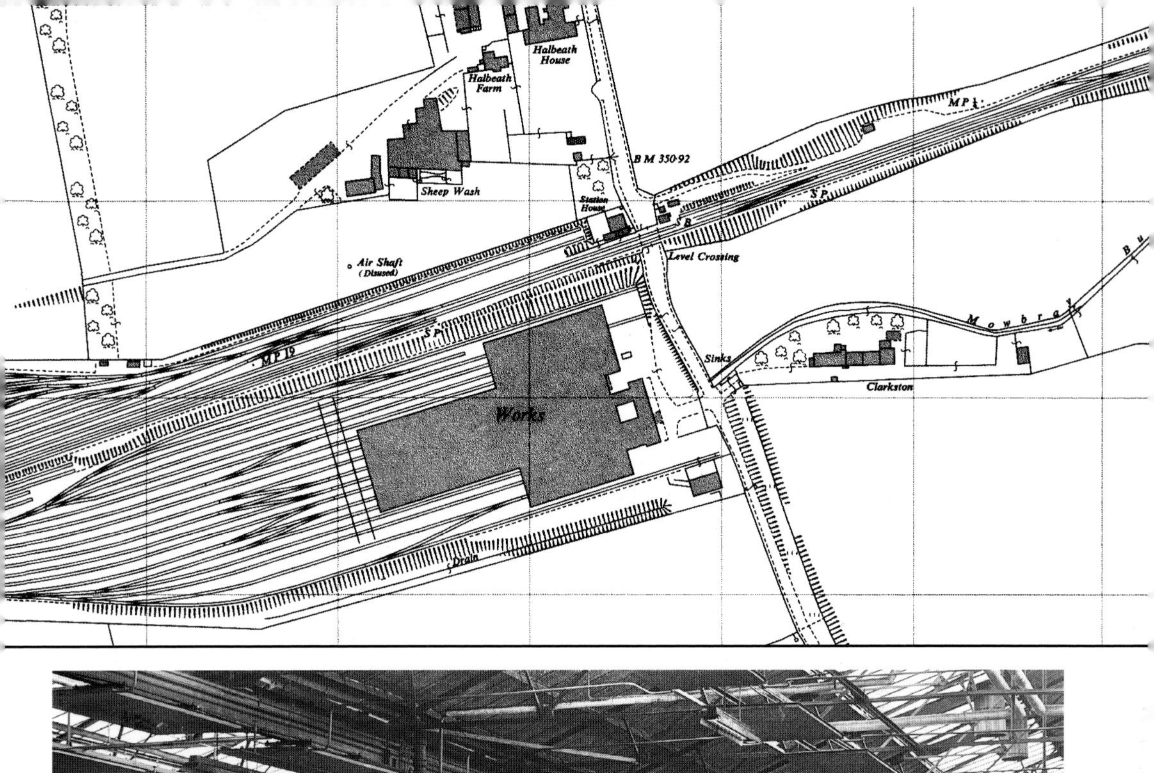
Halbeath House
Halbeath Farm
B M 350·92
Sheep Wash
Station House
Air Shaft
(Disused)
Level Crossing
S P
MP 19
Works
Sinks
Clarkston
Mowbray
Drain

20007

08341
08452

HALBEATH

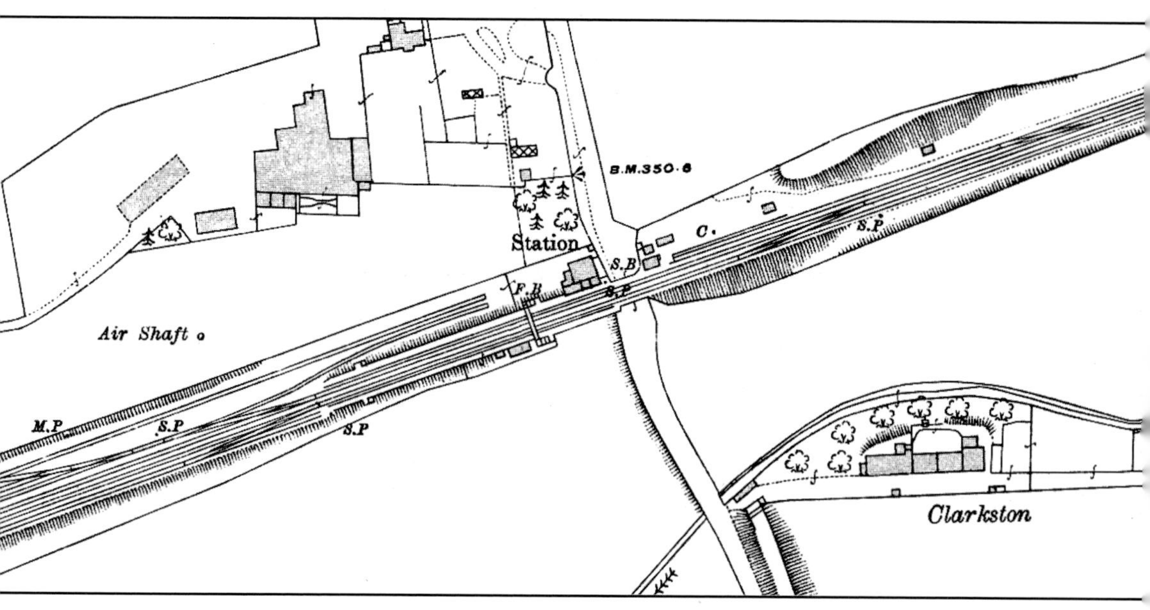

XIV. Seen here in 1913, the station is believed to have been opened with the line on 13th December 1849. It was closed temporarily during World War I from 1st January 1917 and reopened on 1st April 1919. The station closed to passenger traffic on 22nd September 1930 and to goods on 28th December 1964. The station building still exists adjacent to the level crossing, which carries a local road to Kingseat.

31. Halbeath is seen here on 17th September 1949, 19 years after closure. (J.Alsop)

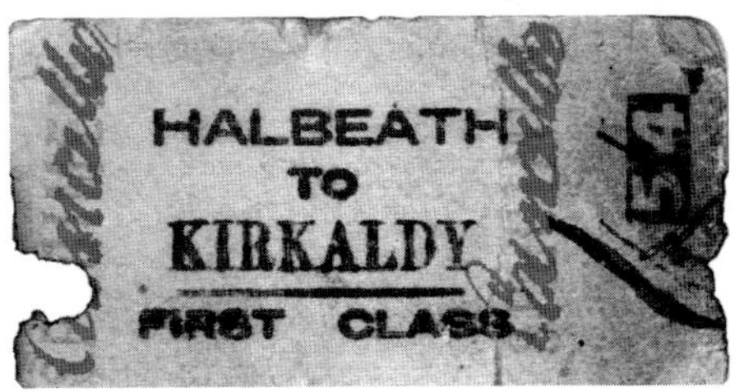

32. The signaller's Morris Minor is parked next to the signal box on 9th April 1971. (*ColourRail.com*)

33. Despite being closed for some 84 years, the station looked in good shape when seen here on 8th May 2014. The crossing gates have been replaced by automatic barriers. (D.A.Lovett)

CROSSGATES

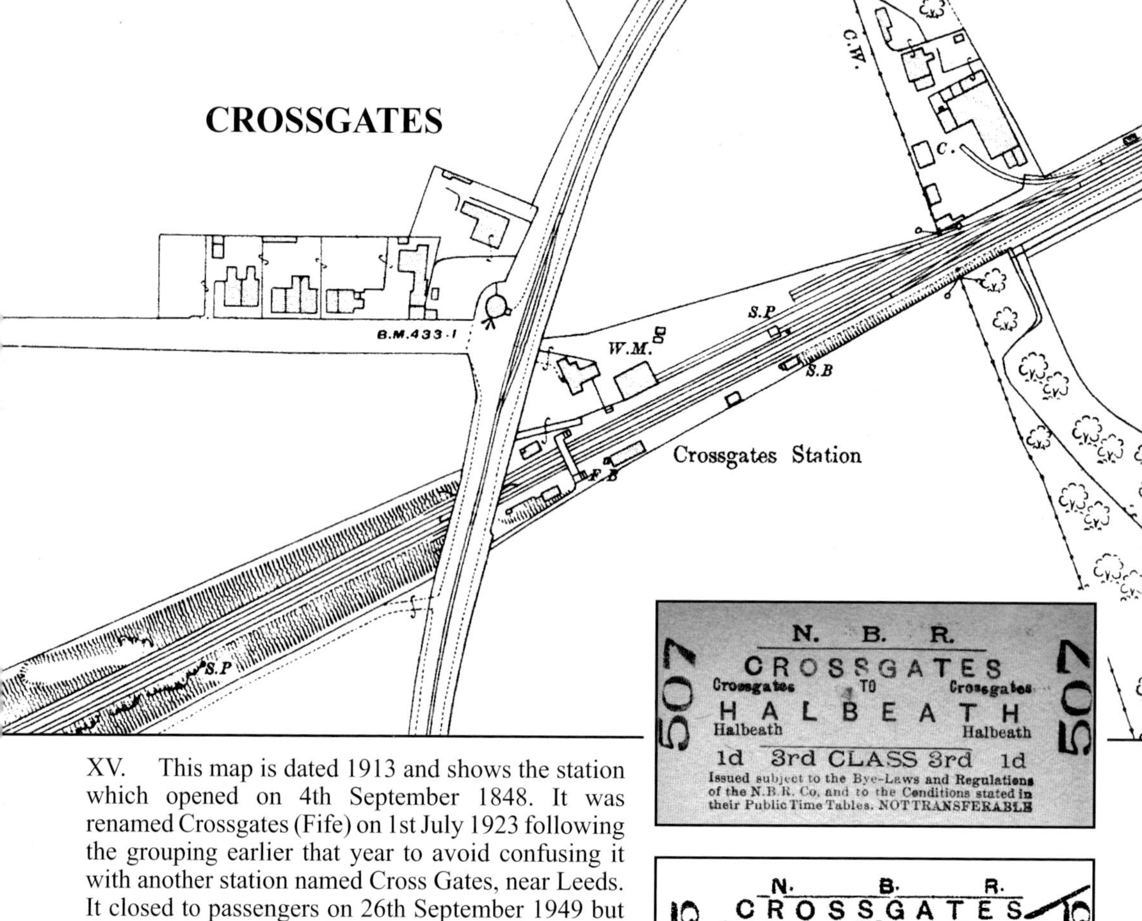

XV. This map is dated 1913 and shows the station which opened on 4th September 1848. It was renamed Crossgates (Fife) on 1st July 1923 following the grouping earlier that year to avoid confusing it with another station named Cross Gates, near Leeds. It closed to passengers on 26th September 1949 but remained open for goods until 10th August 1964.

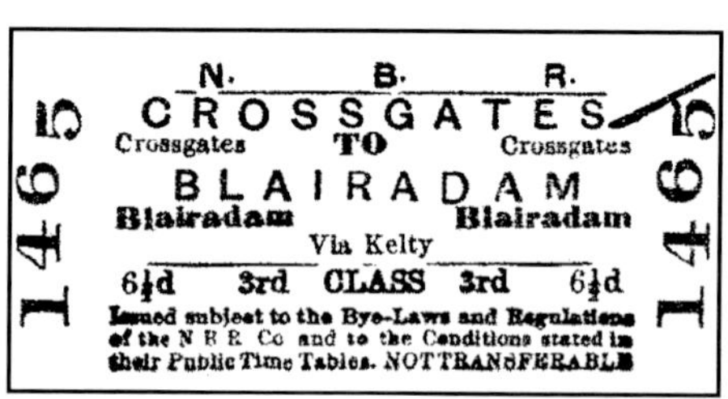

34. The station staff pose for the photographer in the early days of the 20th Century with the staff looking resplendent in their North British Railway uniforms. (A.Brotchie coll.)

35. The platforms have been cut back but the buildings remained in this 1950s view. (C.J.B.Sanderson/Armstrong Trust)

36. GWR Castle class 4-6-0 no. 5043 *Earl of Mount Edgcumbe* passes the site of Crossgates (Fife) station on 27th May 2012 with 'The Caledonian'. (W.Roberton)

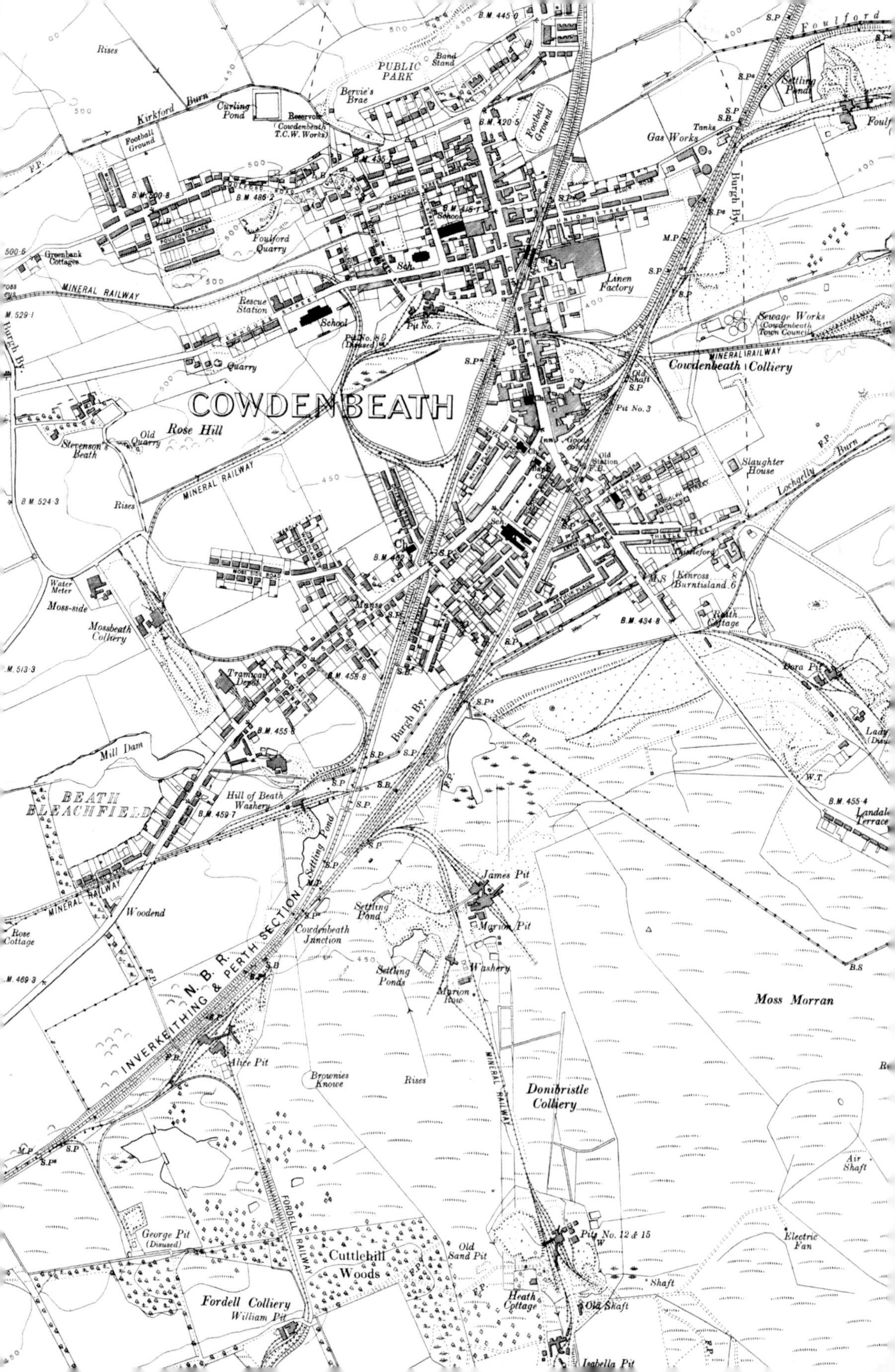
COWDENBEATH
Public Park
Band Stand
Bervie's Brae
Kirkford Burn
Curling Pond
Reservoir (Cowdenbeath T.C.W. Works)
Football Ground
Foulford Quarry
Greenbank Cottages
Mineral Railway
Rescue Station
School
Pit No. 8 (Disused)
Pit No. 7
Football Ground
Gas Works
Tanks
Settling Ponds
Union Street
Linen Factory
Sewage Works (Cowdenbeath Town Council)
Cowdenbeath Colliery
Old Shaft
Pit No. 3
Old Station
Slaughter House
Lochgelly Burn
Thistleford
Kinross
Burntisland
Heath Cottage
Dora Pit
Landale Terrace
Rose Hill
Old Quarry
Stevenson's Beath
Rises
Quarry
Water Meter
Moss-side
Mossbeath Colliery
Manse
Tramway Depot
Mill Dam
Beath Bleachfield
Hill of Beath Washery
Burgh By.
Settling Pond
James Pit
Marion Pit
Washery
Marion Row
Settling Ponds
Woodend
Rose Cottage
Cowdenbeath Junction
N. B. R. Inverkeithing & Perth Section
Alice Pit
Brownies Knowe
Moss Morran
Donibristle Colliery
Mineral Railway
Air Shaft
Electric Fan
Fordell Railway
George Pit (Disused)
Cuttlehill Woods
Old Sand Pit
Pits No. 12 & 15
Shaft
Old Shaft
Heath Cottage
Fordell Colliery
William Pit
Isabella Pit

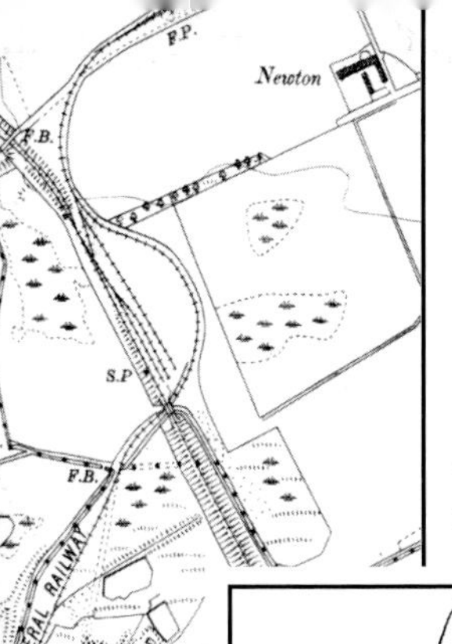

2. Cowdenbeath South Junction to Thornton Junction via Cowdenbeath Old

Cowdenbeath Area

← XVI. This 1913 map, derived from a 6in to one mile map, shows many of the area's collieries.

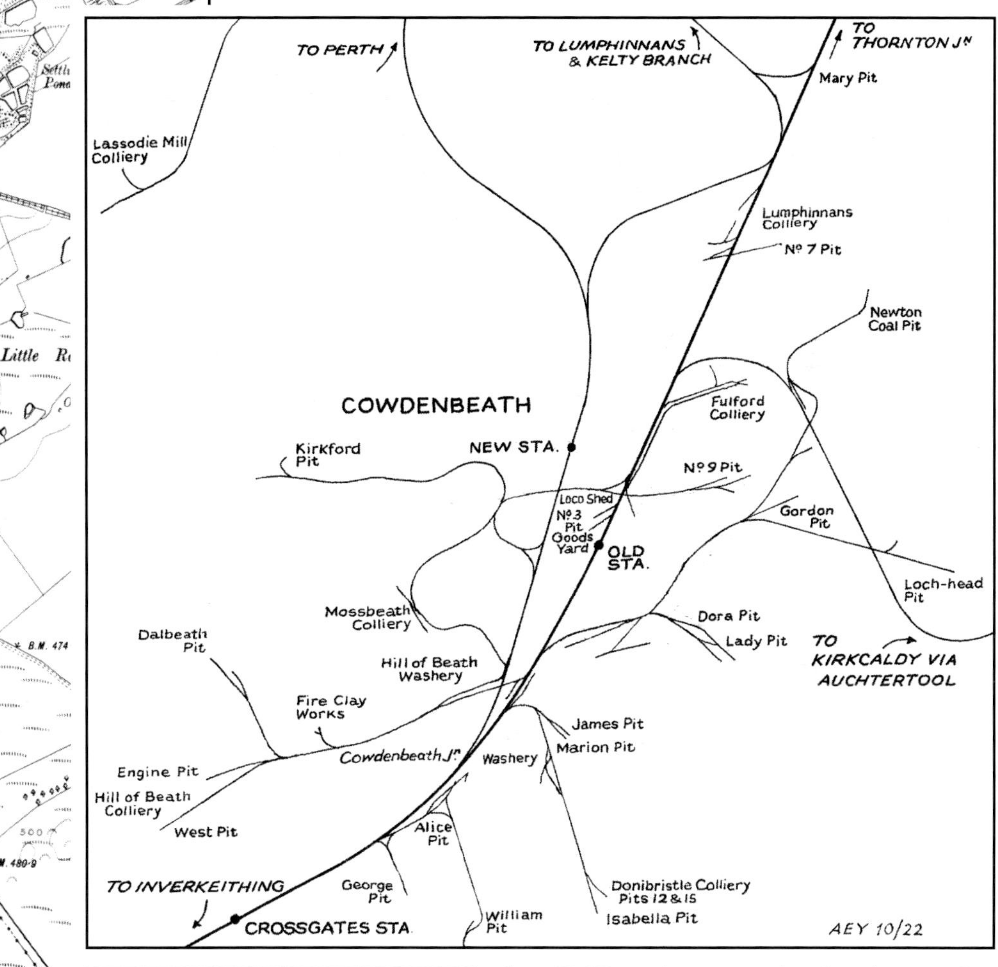

↑ XVII. Area map showing the complex of lines to collieries and their relationship to the two stations. (A.E.Young)

George Pit

← *(Inset)* XVIII. The short branch that served George Pit is seen here in 1896. Opened in 1850, it was originally connected to the Fordell Railway, also connected to Edinburgh, Perth & Dundee using mixed gauge track. This allowed coal to be transported via either route. The pit was closed by 1913.

Alice Pit

37. The branch to George Pit is connected to the Alice Pit complex. Alice Pit was originally served by the Fordell Tramway to St David's Harbour. Situated in the Crossgates area, Fordell Colliery comprised three pits near to each other. Alice (no. 1 pit), William (no. 2 pit) and Lady Anne (no. 3 pit). Alice pit opened in 1894 and closed in 1966. (A.Brotchie coll.)

William Pit

38. William Pit was connected to Alice Pit. It opened in 1845 and closed in 1950. An interesting selection of ancient coal waggons are seen in this early 20th Century view. (A Brotchie coll.)

Lady Anne Pit

39. Lady Anne (no. 3 pit) was part of the Fordell complex and was served by the railway of the same name. It opened in 1830 and closed in 1966 before being finally abandoned in 1970. At its peak in 1959 it employed 622. (A.Brotchie coll.)

Cowdenbeath South Junction

40. Cowdenbeath South Junction is shown in map XVI on page 34 (marked Cowdenbeath Junction). This is where after 1890 the line to Cowdenbeath New station left the original line through Cowdenbeath, the earlier station becoming known as Cowdenbeath Old. The new station was built as part of the Forth Bridge works and created a new main line to Perth over Glenfarg.

Cowdenbeath South Junction signal box stands in the space between the old line (in the background) and the 1890 built new line to Cowdenbeath New station. It is seen here in around 1980 after a great deal of rationalisation had taken place.

The later double line on the left heads north towards New station and the connections to the various pits to the west of Cowdenbeath. These will feature in a future album.

Following the opening of the new station in 1890 and the closure of the old in 1919 to passenger traffic, the original line served as a loop for goods traffic, mainly coal. The line was gradually reduced in status during the 1960s with the section between the tunnel and Lumphinnans Central Junction closing in 1966; the remaining section continued to serve the NCB Central Workshops. Dora opencast mine was established in the early 1970s, continuing production until 1984, the line latterly operating as a siding. Our journey continues over the original line via Cowdenbeath Old. The route through Cowdenbeath New appears later in this album. (Scottish Railway Preservation Society)

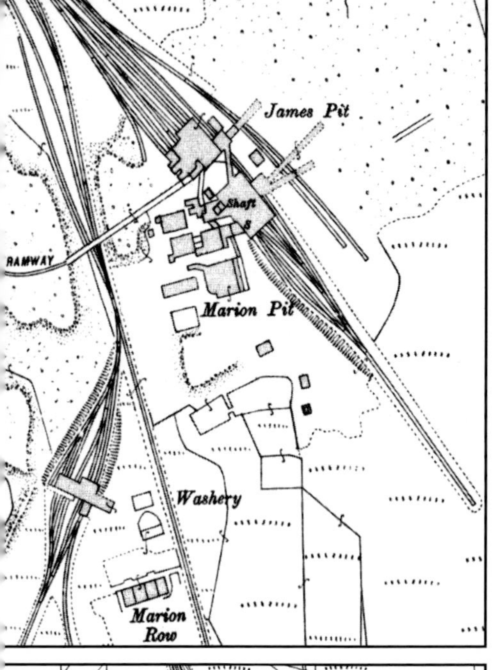

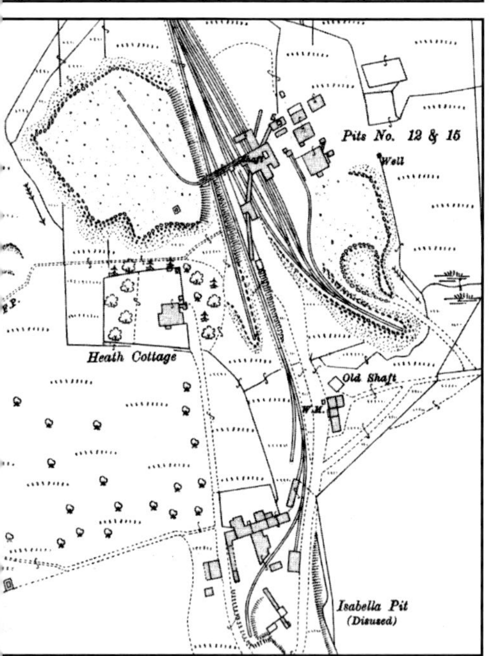

James Pit & Marion Pit

A branch line ran south east to serve James Pit, Marion Pit and Isabella Pit, which all operated under the auspices of Donibristle Colliery.

XIX. The two pits, James and Marion, were located next to each other. James Pit opened in 1874 and closed around 1933. Operated initially by Grieve & Naysmith, it was taken over by Donibristle Colliery Company in 1890 and became part of the Fife Coal Company in 1915. Marion Pit also opened in 1874 and closed in 1933. It too became part of the Fife Coal Company. The map is dated 1913.

Foulford Colliery and Cowdenbeath Central Washery

The Central Washery was located to the west of Marion Pit on the line to the Donibristle Pits as seen on the previous 1913 map.

Originally Foulford Colliery No. 1 pit, it was opened in 1884 by the Cowdenbeath Coal Company. No. 2 pit was opened in 1924 by the Fife Coal Company who took over Foulford in 1899. Both were closed in 1931.

The Central Washery remained open until closure in 1961.

Donibristle Colliery Pits 12 & 15 and Isabella Pit

XX. This was the layout of Donibristle Colliery (also known as Donibristle 12/15 Pits) in 1913. Opened in 1830, it closed in 1933. There was a short-lived pit known as Ashley Pit between 1842 and 1851.

Donibristle was operated by Grieve & Naysmith and taken over by Donibristle Colliery Company in 1890. It became part of the Fife Coal Company in 1911.

Isabella Pit (also known as No.8 Pit) opened in 1838 and closed in 1895. It continued in use as a pumping station for Donibristle Colliery

Junction north east to Dora Pit & Lady Pit line splits to Gordon Pit, Loch-head Pit and Newton Pit

Seen centre-right in the large map, no. XVI, Dora Pit opened in 1875 and closed in 1959. At its peak in 1958 it employed 280 people.

From 1974, open cast mining took place to remove coal stocks just below the surface, much of it being moved by rail to Longannet Power Station. Coal was taken out by train using the remaining section of the line from Cowdenbeath South Junction via Cowdenbeath Old. Trains came to an end around 1982. The former open cast site is now Lumphinnans Golf Course following a major reclamation project.

Lady Pit (which became part of Little Raith Colliery) opened in 1855 and closed in 1898. It was operated by The Lochgelly Iron & Coal Company.

41. NCB No. 37, an Andrew Barclay 0-4-0ST built in 1912, is seen here working hard out of Dora Colliery in August 1958. It is passing the NCB engine shed. (H.Townley/Industrial Railway Society)

42. Class 20 nos 20224 and 20202 are at Dora Sidings, Cowdenbeath, on 8th April 1977 during the days of open cast mining. (H.Stevenson)

Gordon Pit & Lochhead Pit

↘*(bottom right)* 43. A view of the headgear and general surface layout of Lochhead Colliery, Beath. This was probably taken following closure, which took place in 1932. (National Mining Museum Scotland)

↓ XXI. Dated 1913, this extract shows the location of both Gordon Pit and the line linking it to Lochhead Pit. Gordon Pit opened in 1893 and closed in 1939, whilst Lochhead Pit opened in 1897 and closed in 1932.

The line running from top to bottom is the Auchtertool line. This linked the Cowdenbeath area to Kirkcaldy, which will be covered in a future album.

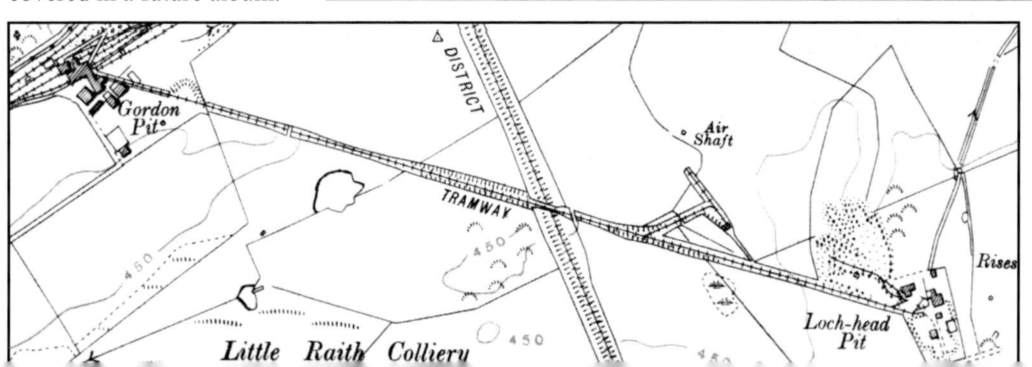

Newton Pit

XXII. This 1913 map shows Newton Pit, which was also known as Arthur Pit. It opened in 1892 and closed in 1925, and was operated by the Lochgelly Iron & Coal Company.

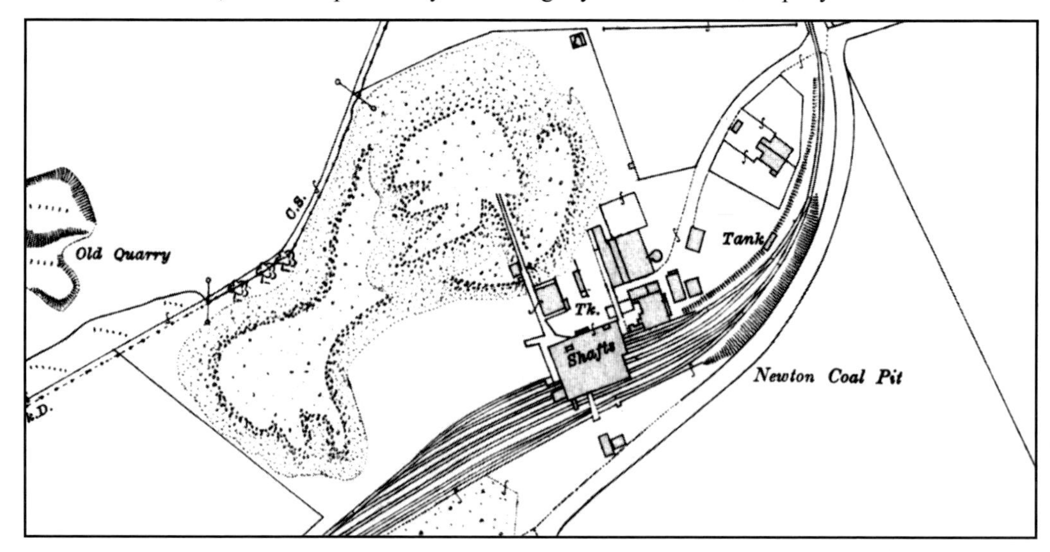

COWDENBEATH OLD

XXIII. Cowdenbeath came into being around 1820 with the railway arriving in 1849. This station (later named Cowdenbeath Old) was the only station in Cowdenbeath until 1890. It is seen here on this 1894 map and was still in use at that time. Opened on 4th September 1848 it was named in *Bradshaw* as Cowdenbeath Junction from 1862 until 1890. It was renamed Cowdenbeath Old from 1st June 1890 but closed on 31st March 1919, although miners' trains continued to call here long after closure to regular passenger trains when Cowdenbeath New became the town's station. Goods traffic was withdrawn on 1st January 1968. The line through the site is now a footpath and cycleway, whilst the area behind the fence is now a car park.

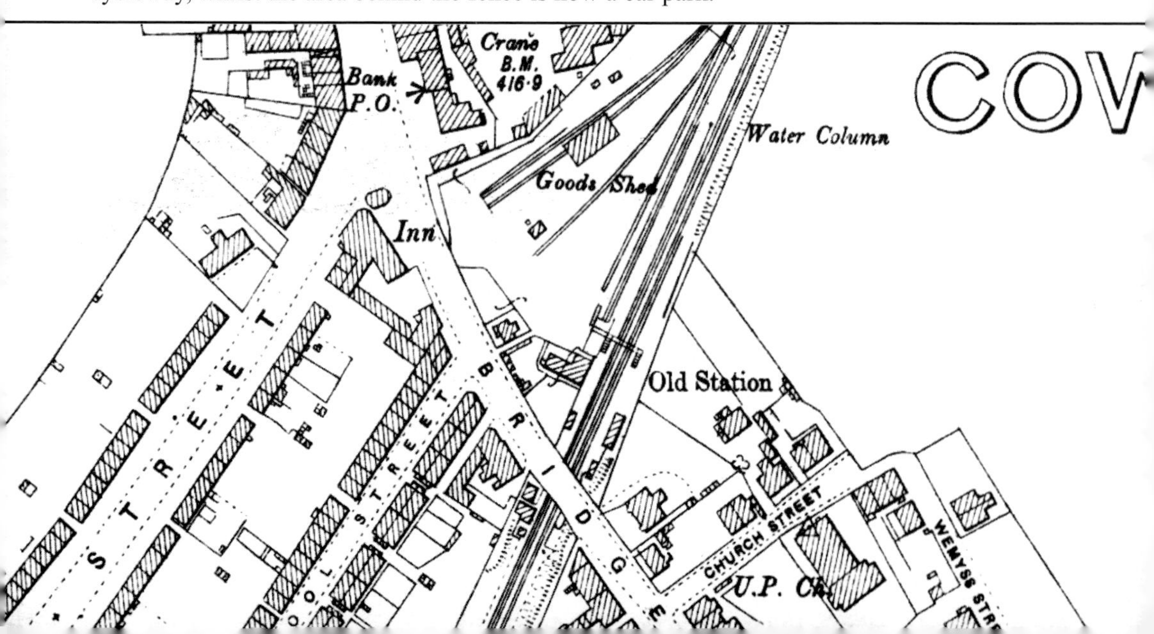

44. Looking southwest from the up platform on 14th July 1955, 36 years after closure to regular passenger traffic. (W.A.Camwell/Stephenson Locomotive Society)

45. Now we look north on 27th February 1960 from underneath the road bridge, which carries Bridge Street over the old line. (W.A.C.Smith/Transport Treasury)

46. Looking south towards Bridge Street. The two distinctive buildings to the right still remain today with the track bed now forming a footpath. The area to the right of the fence posts is now a car park. (H.Stevenson)

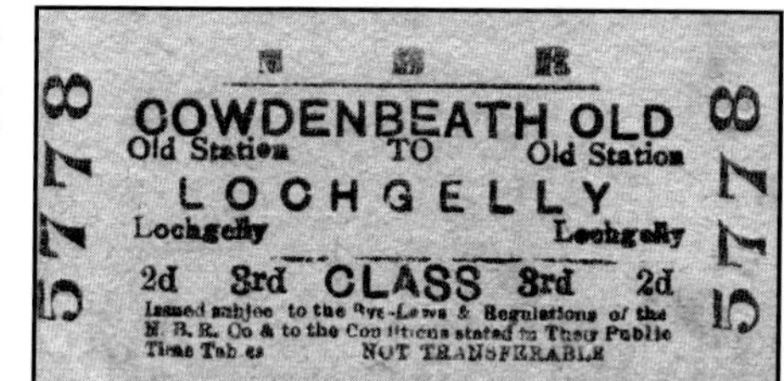

47. This southward view, dated October 1971, shows the Central Workshops to the right of the track, which is now looking somewhat overgrown. (J.L.Stevenson)

48. With the Dora opencast loading site on the right we are looking north to the now buried tunnel that once carried the line towards Lumphinnans Central Junction. On 28th August 1976 the Branch Line Society ran a rail tour along the line, which allowed those travelling to inspect the available facilities. (W.Roberton)

← 49. A three-car class 101 DMU stands at the former station site whilst passengers walk towards the tunnel, seen in the previous picture, during the 1976 Branch Line Society rail tour. (W.Roberton)

Cowdenbeath No. 3 Pit

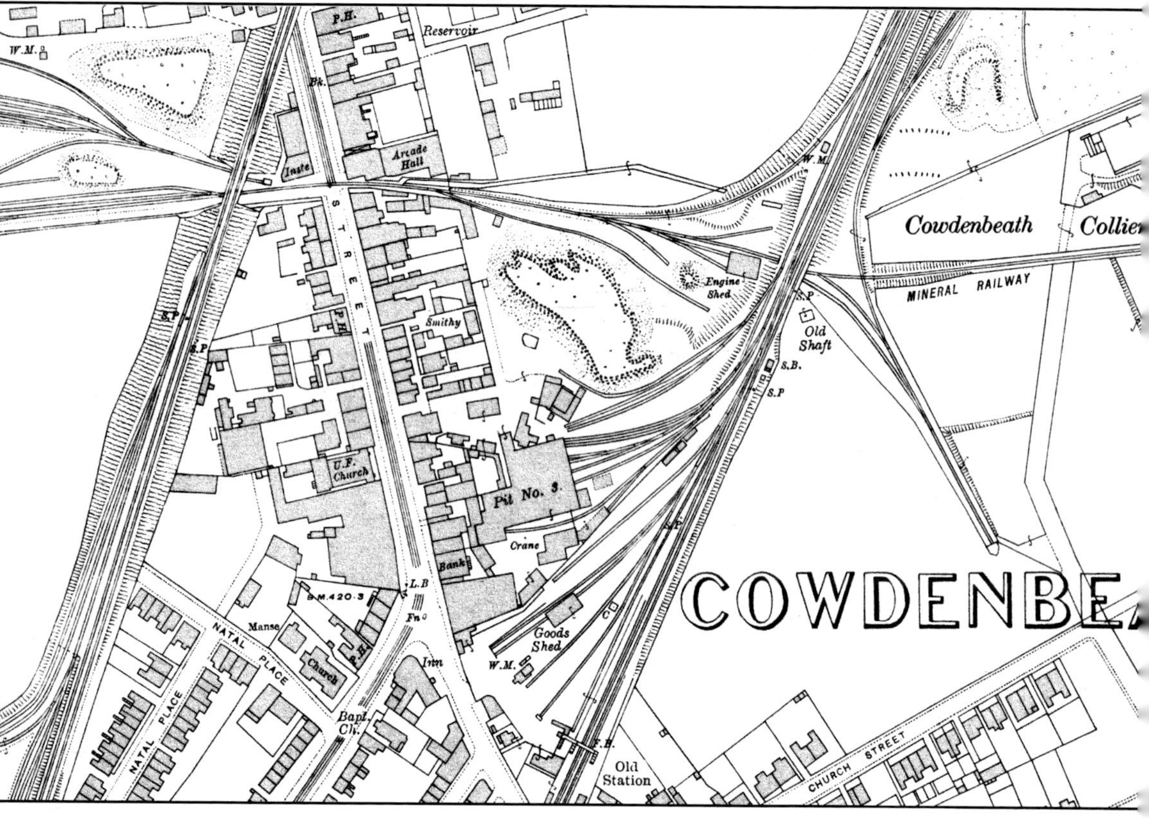

XXIV. No. 3 Pit was located just north of the old station as seen here in 1913. It opened in 1896 and closed in 1925.

Cowdenbeath NCB Loco Shed

50. Seen in the map above, is the former two-road engine shed, which continued in use until the end of steam traction in the National Coal Board Fife Area. In later years, as the photographs reveal, it was looking somewhat neglected. It continued to be the operational base for the 'Pug' locomotive used to move stock around the Central Workshops.

Andrew Barclay no. 54 0-4-0ST was built in 1901. It is seen here outside the engine shed on 15th June 1966. (B.Roberts/ Industrial Railway Society)

51. Seen here around 1968, only one road into the shed still retained rails. The line passing over the bridge is the old main line through Cowdenbeath old station. The line passing underneath went on to serve Cowdenbeath Central Works and Cowdenbeath No. 9 pit. (P.Westwater)

Cowdenbeath NCB Central Works

XXV. The Central Works dominates the centre of this 6in to one mile map dated 1938. The Central Works were built in 1924 by the Fife Coal Company on a site covering 17¾ acres. It provided office accommodation for management, laboratories, equipment and material stores, as well as workshops for the maintenance of equipment, including locomotives and rolling stock. At its peak it employed some 750 people. Following closure of many mines in the 1980s, the Central Workshops, the last National Coal workshops to remain open, closed in December 1988 despite a sustained fight to retain it. The buildings subsequently became a local industrial estate. It is now scheduled for major redevelopment that will involve the demolition of the remaining buildings.

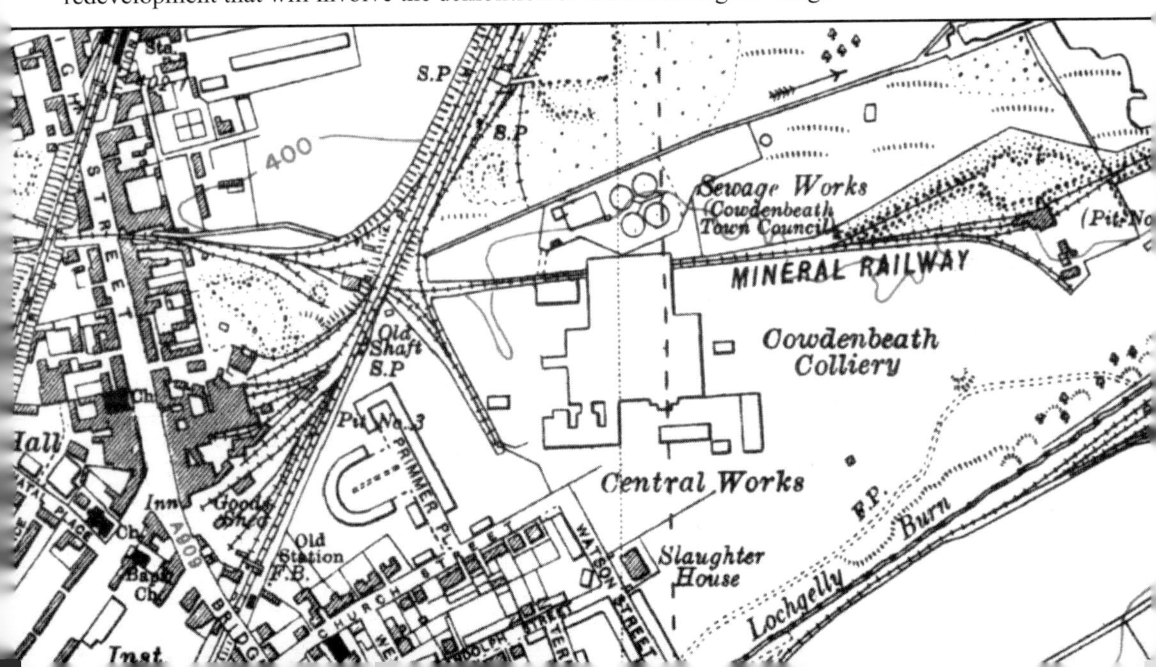

52. Fife Coal Co. Ltd No. 18 0-4-0ST Barclay & Co. no. 275, built in 1880, is being stripped at the Central Works on 24th July 1937. It was originally built for Oakley Colliery Co in Fife and was taken over by the Fife Coal Co. in 1924, and was officially scrapped in 1935. (E.S.Lomax/Stephenson Locomotive Society)

53. The branch alongside the Central Workshops is seen here in the mid-1960s. (P.Westwater)

➔ 54. A visit to the Central Workshops in Church Street, Cowdenbeath would often reveal a number of locomotives and wagons awaiting overhaul or scrapping. Seen here on 19th February 1968 is resident works locomotive NCB No. 43 Fife Area shunting wagons under the watchful eye of workshop staff. No. 43 was preserved and is now cared for by the Shed 47 Railway Restoration Group, which is based at Lathalmond, also the home of The Scottish Vintage Bus Museum. (H.Stevenson)

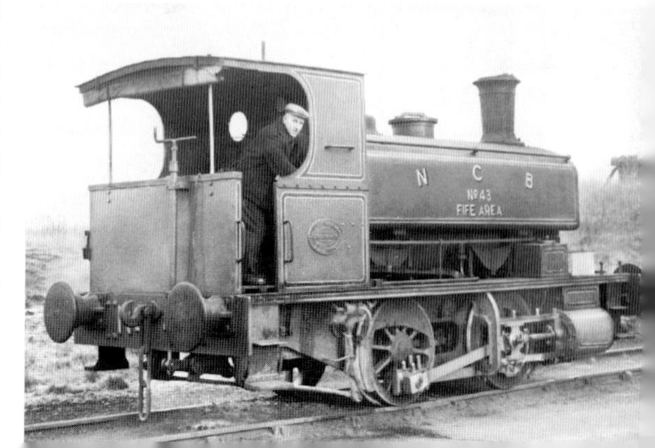

55. The NCB Cowdenbeath Central Workshops, seen from the Cowdenbeath (Old) line in 1976. Andrew Barclay 0-6-0T 1296 of 1915 is in the centre of the picture. The locomotive finished its working life at Polkemmet Colliery. (W.Roberton)

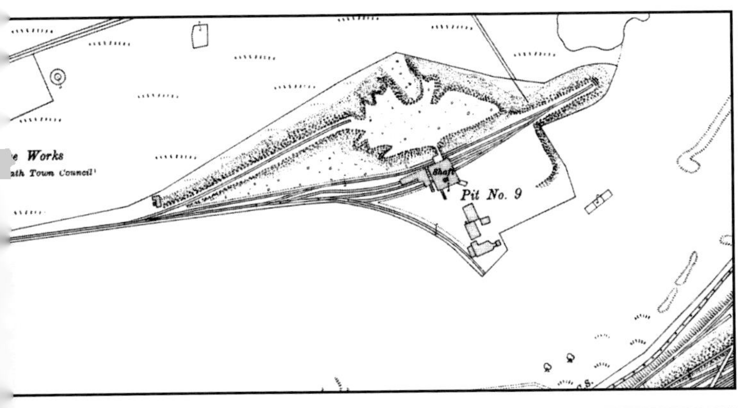

Cowdenbeath No. 9 Pit

XXVI. Cowdenbeath No 9 pit was sunk in 1894 and closed in 1925. Gordon Pit is in the bottom right-hand corner of this 1913 map.

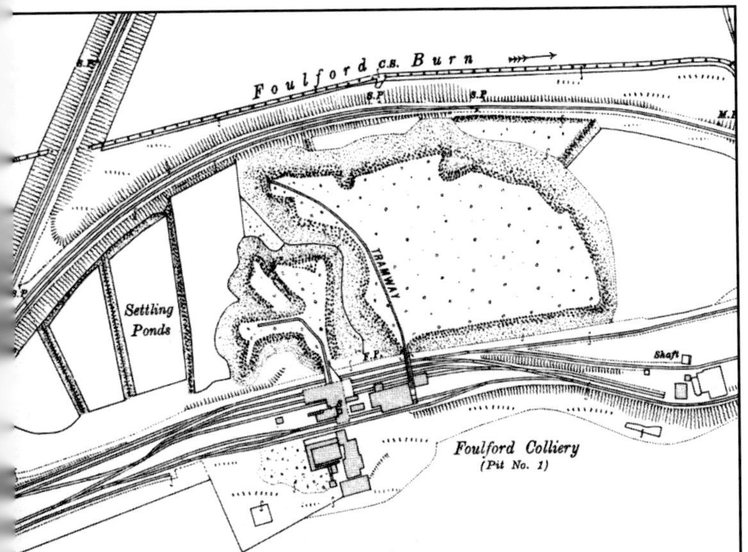

Foulford Colliery and Foulford Junction

XXVII. This 1913 map shows the branch east to Foulford colliery, which was linked to Cowdenbeath No. 9 pit. Opened in 1884 by the Cowdenbeath Coal Co, it was operated by the Fife Coal Co. from 1896. No. 2 shaft was sunk in 1924. It closed in 1931, remaining in use as a washery only until the mid-1950s. The site is now buried underneath Cowdenbeath Golf Course.

56. Following its closure, the washery continued taking in coal from other Cowdenbeath pits, which would account for the huge bings. Foulford Junction box can be seen near the gas holder controlling the junction for the former Kirkcaldy District Railway line, via Auchtertool. The roofs of the Central Workshops can also be seen in the view looking back towards Cowdenbeath, with a permanent way trolley occupying the up line. (Scottish Railway Preservation Society)

57. Foulford Junction signal box is seen here on 5th March 1962. War Department 2-8-0 no. 90020 heads towards Cowdenbeath. Behind the locomotive, the Auchtertool line heads off to the right, whilst in the foreground is a link to the lines serving Foulford Colliery. (W.S.Sellar)

Cowdenbeath No. 7 Pit

XXVIII. Seen here on this 1913 map, Cowdenbeath No. 7 pit opened in 1860 and closed 100 years later in 1960. At its peak in 1950 it employed 454.

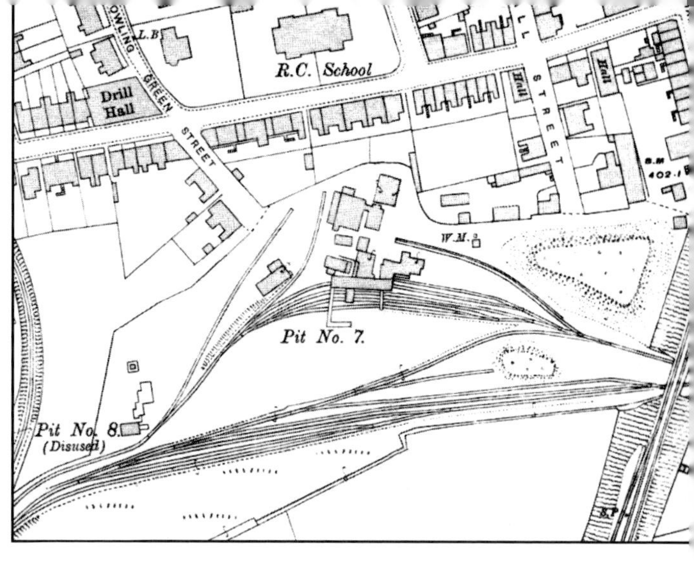

↓ 58. NCB 0-4-0ST No. 20, built by Grant Ritchie in 1890, appears to be out of use at Cowdenbeath No. 7 colliery in August 1958. (H.Townley/ Industrial Railway Society)

Lumphinnans Colliery No. 1

↙ *(bottom)* 59. Located on the west side of the Dunfermline-Thornton line, No.1 pit was accessed via Lumphinnans Colliery Junction. It opened initially in 1826 as an ironstone pit, becoming a colliery in 1852. Taken over by Fife Coal Company in 1896, it had previously been operated by Oakley Iron Company and Cowdenbeath Coal Company. At its peak in 1951 it employed 202 before closure in 1957. It can be seen on the bottom half of map XXIX, on the following page. The 1890 line from Cowdenbeath North Junction can be seen bottom left heading for Lumphinnans Central Junction. This is the only line remaining today.

The image shows Fife Coal Company 0-4-0ST No. 14. at Lumphinnans No. 1 colliery on 6th August 1938. Works no. 146 was built in 1890. In the background, wagons of the Fife Coal Company are being loaded. (E.S.Lomax/ Stephenson Locomotive Society)

Lumphinnans Central Junction

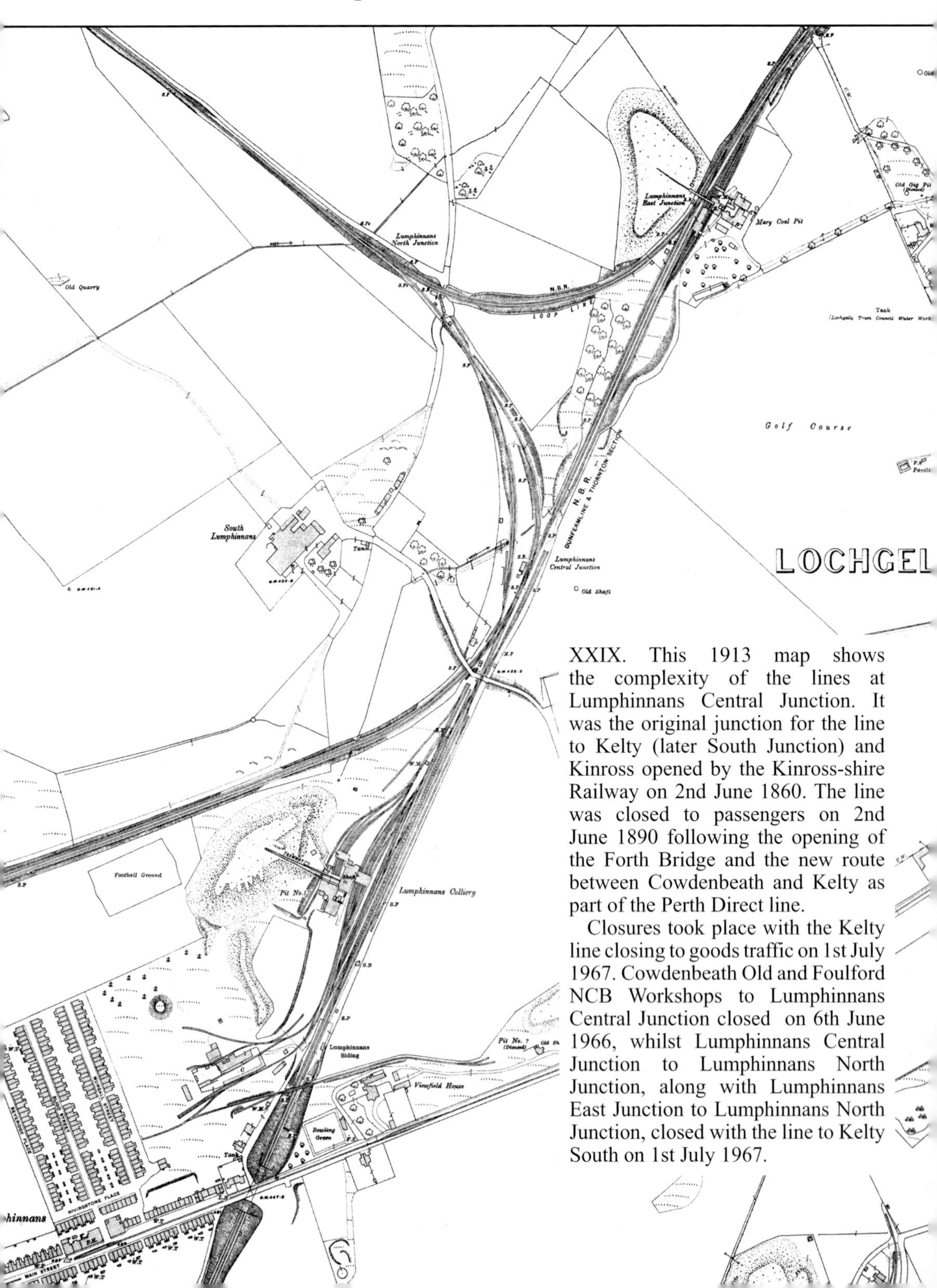

XXIX. This 1913 map shows the complexity of the lines at Lumphinnans Central Junction. It was the original junction for the line to Kelty (later South Junction) and Kinross opened by the Kinross-shire Railway on 2nd June 1860. The line was closed to passengers on 2nd June 1890 following the opening of the Forth Bridge and the new route between Cowdenbeath and Kelty as part of the Perth Direct line.

Closures took place with the Kelty line closing to goods traffic on 1st July 1967. Cowdenbeath Old and Foulford NCB Workshops to Lumphinnans Central Junction closed on 6th June 1966, whilst Lumphinnans Central Junction to Lumphinnans North Junction, along with Lumphinnans East Junction to Lumphinnans North Junction, closed with the line to Kelty South on 1st July 1967.

60. LNER D49 class 4-4-0 no. 62712 *Morayshire* hauls the 1.52pm Thornton Junction to Dunfermline Lower service past Lumphinnans Central Junction on 27th January 1960. The line to Kelty passes behind the signal box on the left of the picture. *Morayshire* was subsequently preserved and is now at the Scottish Railway Preservation Society site at Bo'ness. (W.A.C.Smith/Transport Treasury)

Lochgelly Area

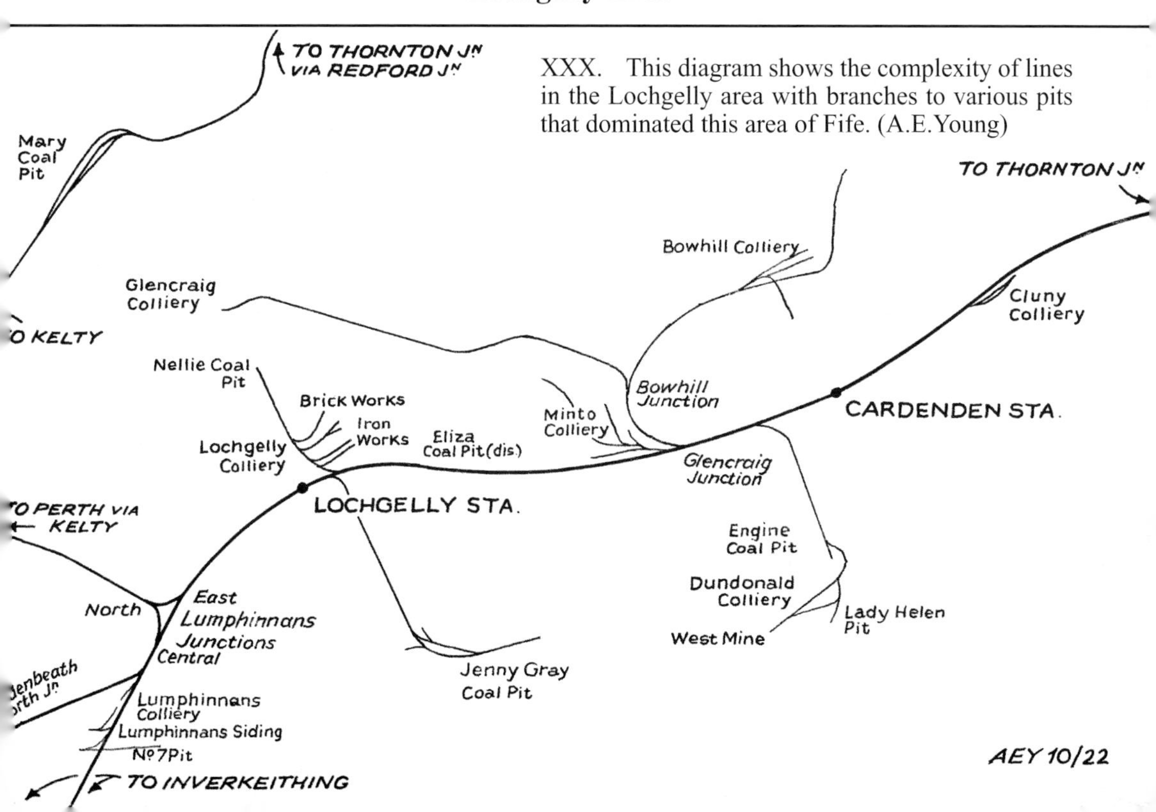

XXX. This diagram shows the complexity of lines in the Lochgelly area with branches to various pits that dominated this area of Fife. (A.E.Young)

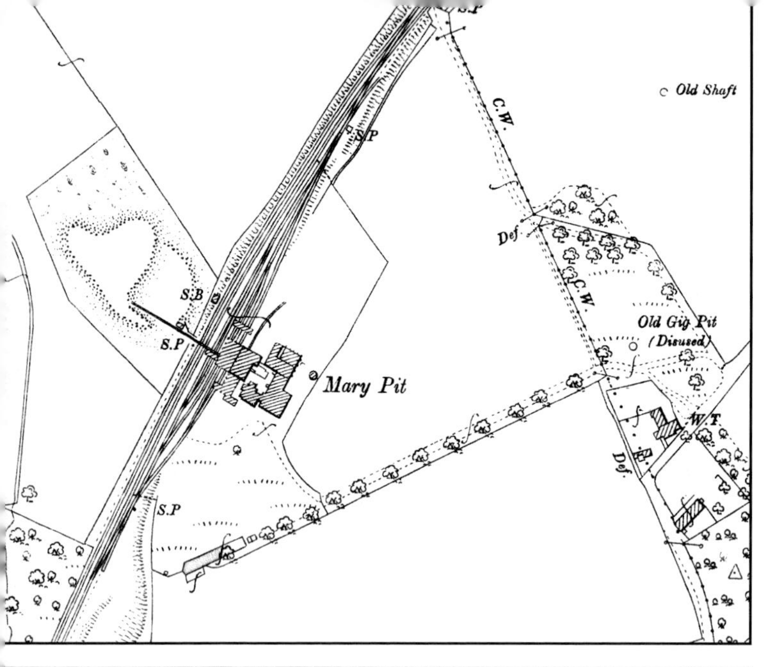

Mary Pit

XXXI. Seen here in 1896 is Mary Pit, which closed in 1928. The name 'Mary' should not be confused with a pit of the same name at nearby Lochore, which was sunk in 1902 and closed in 1966. The pit head wheel is now displayed in the Lochore Country Park, located on the old pit site.

LOCHGELLY

XXXII. This map dates from 1947 and shows the station, which had opened 99 years earlier on 4th September 1848. The town takes its name from Loch Gelly, which lies a mile to the southeast of the town centre. Its population in 1960 was 9,388.

Although the station lost its goods facilities on 5th October 1964, it just about remained open during the 1970s. Lochgelly was only served by morning and evening peak trains that terminated at Cardenden. From 15th May 1989 the line between Cardenden and Thornton South Junction regained its passenger services.

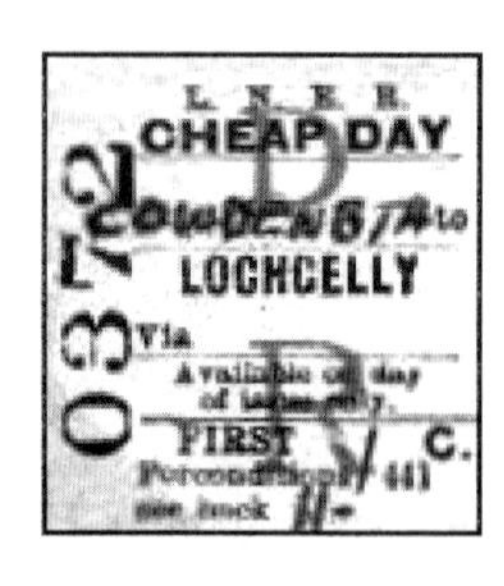

61. The main station building was located on the up platform. The goods yard and gas works were located behind the building. (W.Lynn coll.)

62. Seen here on 9th September 1978, the platforms straddled the bridge over Station Road and were slightly staggered as a result. (A.E.Young)

63. A very sad looking station is seen here on 9th September 1978, during the time when it was served by a peak-hours only service. (A.E.Young)

64. On the same day, the approach road to the station shows dereliction setting in. (A.E.Young)

65. The approach road shows a more modest shelter in place of the station building, with the booking office now replaced with a ticket machine. This view is dated 16th October 2008. (D.A.Lovett)

66. We look in the direction of Cowdenbeath on the same day. The station building has been demolished and the footbridge removed. The down platform has been extended. (D.A.Lovett)

67. The photographer is looking towards Thornton Junction on 16th October 2008. The extended up platform reflects the growth in traffic since the introduction of Fife Circle services in 1989. (D.A.Lovett)

Jenny Gray Pit

Just after the station a branch to the south served the Jenny Gray Pit.

XXXIII. This 1947 map shows the mineral line leading from the main line to Jenny Gray pit. Opened in 1854 it was part of the Lochgelly Iron & Coal Company and was linked to the main line by a rope-worked incline. Its peak year was 1950 when it employed 492. It closed in 1959.

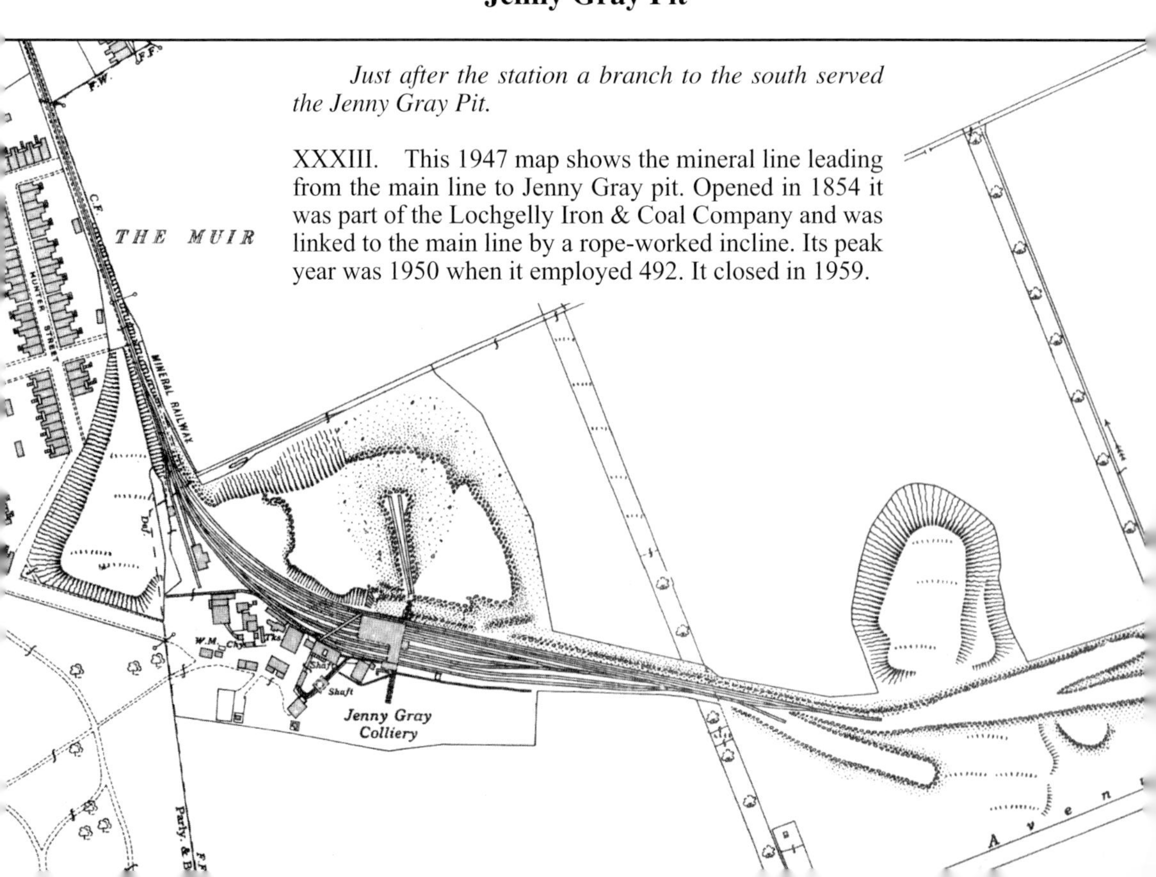

68. A general view of the Jenny Gray Pit showing some of the sidings. (J.Peden/Industrial Railway Society)

Branch to Iron Works, Brickworks & Nellie Coal Pit

XXXIV. A further branch ran to the north, as shown here in 1947, which served an Iron Works, the Lochgelly Tile & Brickworks and Nellie Pit (Lochgelly Colliery). The Iron Works existed between 1846 and 1895. The Tile & Brickworks was also in use by 1846, but continued in production until 1970.

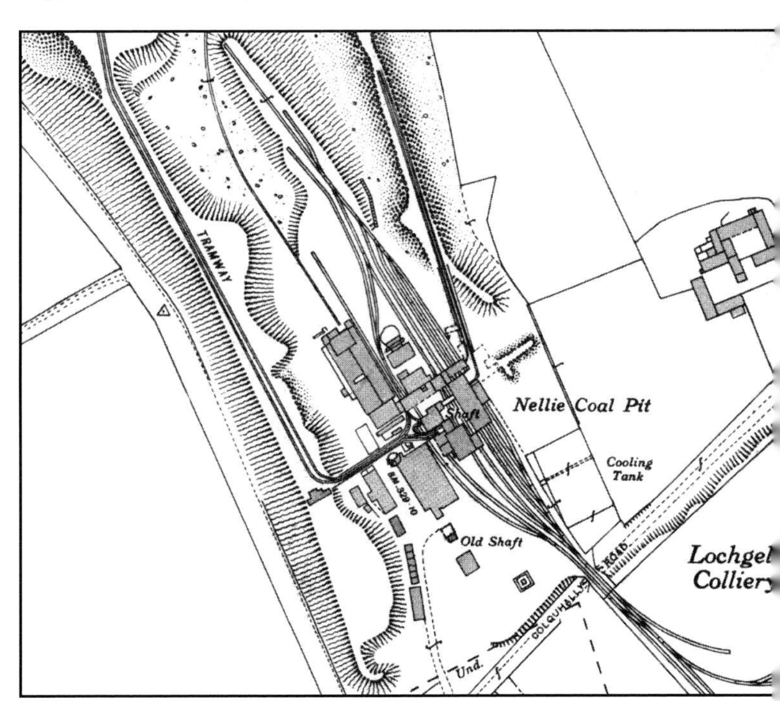

69. Lochgelly Iron & Co. Ltd Andrew Barclay 0-4-0ST (works no. 727 of 1894) No. 8 is seen here on 22nd May 1939. (E.S.Lomax/Stephenson Locomotive Society)

Nellie Pit (Lochgelly Colliery)

The branch that served the Tile & Brickworks continued to Nellie Pit, also known as Lochgelly Colliery. Opened in 1880, its peak year was 1958 when it employed 508. It closed in 1965.

70. Lochgelly No. 5 poses for the camera at Nellie Pit (Lochgelly Colliery) in around 1900. It was an 0-4-0ST, built by Andrew Barclay at Kilmarnock in 1879 as works no. 202. (J.Alsop coll.)

Eliza Coal Pit

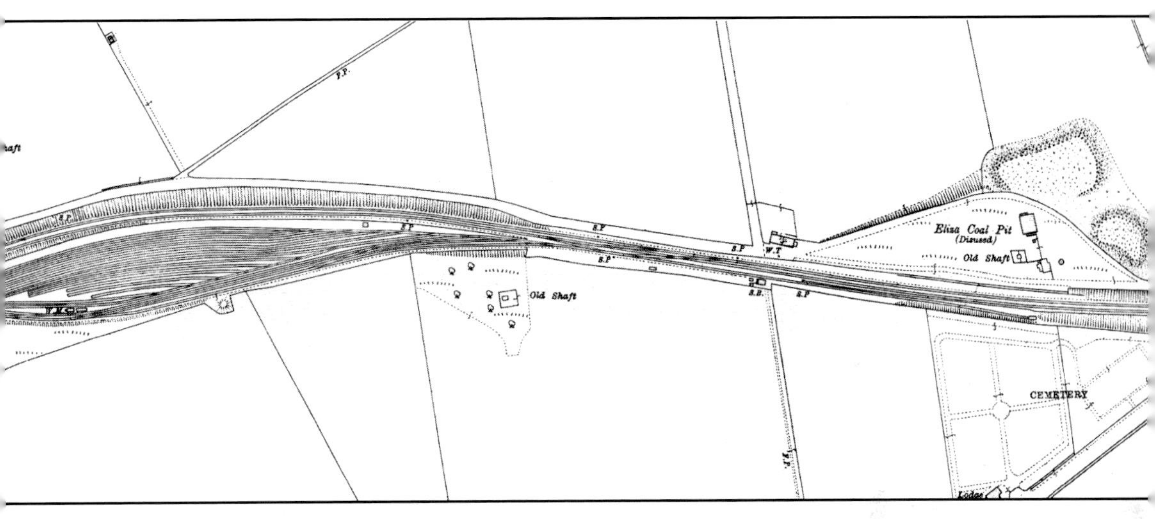

XXXV. Eliza Pit opened circa 1870 and closed due to flooding in around 1886. Not surprisingly it appears on this 1913 map as still being disused.

Minto Pit, Glencraig Junction and Bowhill Junction

XXXVI. Seen here in 1947, Minto Pit opened in 1903 and closed in 1967. At its peak in 1957 it employed 730. The line from Glencraig Junction on the main line splits at Bowhill Junction to serve Glencraig Colliery, to the left, and Bowhill Colliery, to the right.

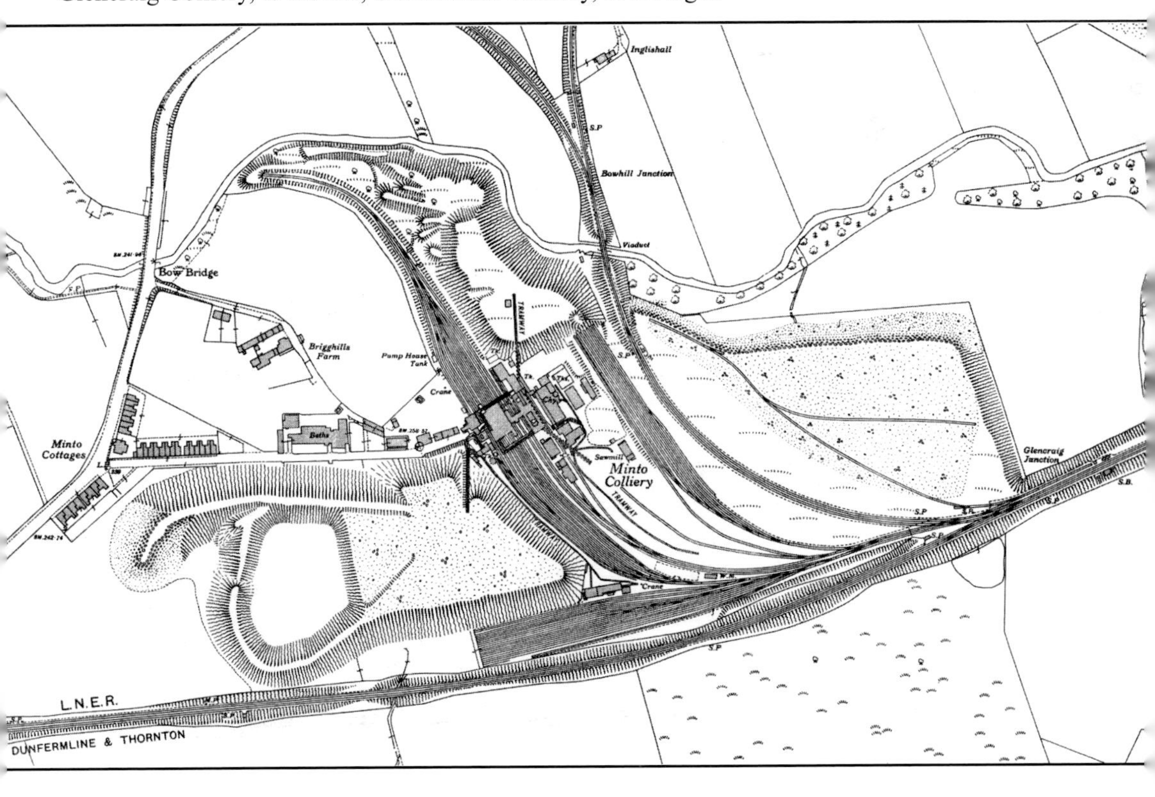

71. A general view of Minto Colliery, Lochgelly, taken in April 1926. Two Lochgelly private owner wagons await loading. (J. Peden/Industrial Railway Society)

Glencraig Junction

72. The signal box at Glencraig Junction is seen here on 17th November 1967. (H.Stevenson)

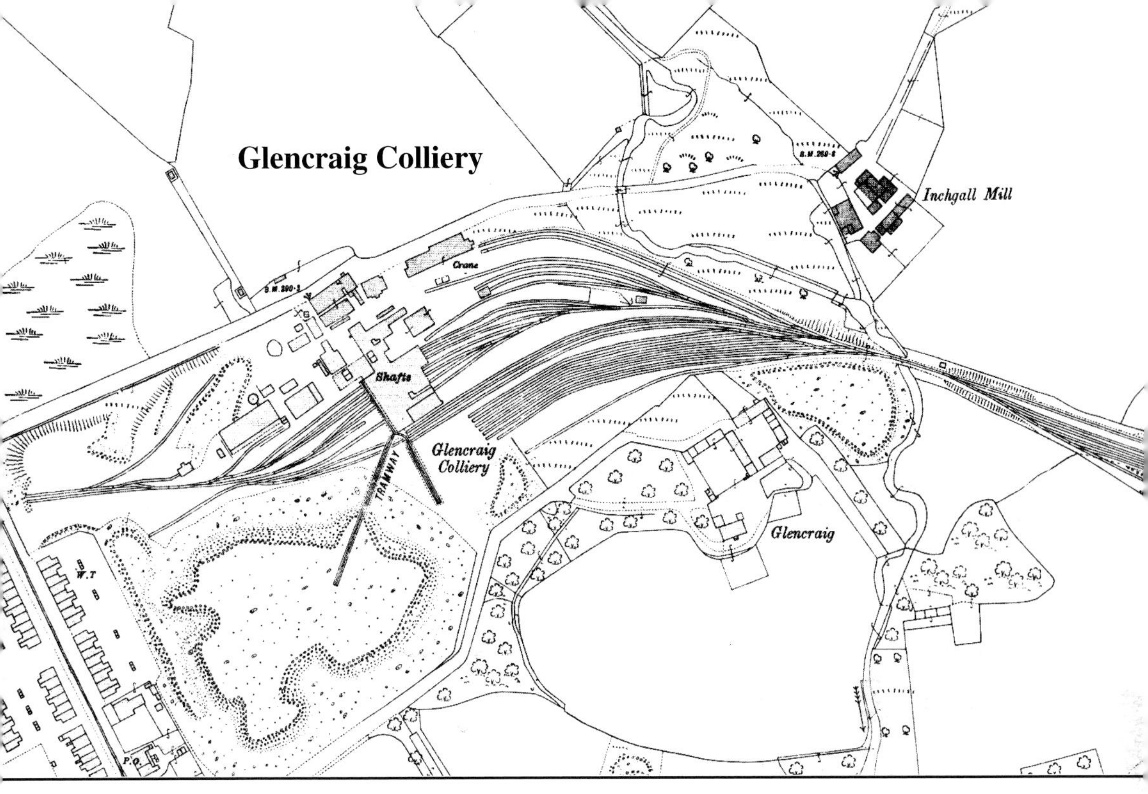

XXXVII. Seen here in 1913, Glencraig Colliery opened in 1896 and closed in 1966. Originally operated by the Wilson & Clyde Coal Company, its peak year was 1950 when 1,316 were employed.

73. This undated general view of the colliery buildings shows private owner wagons being loaded with coal. (Jim Peden/Industrial Railway Society)

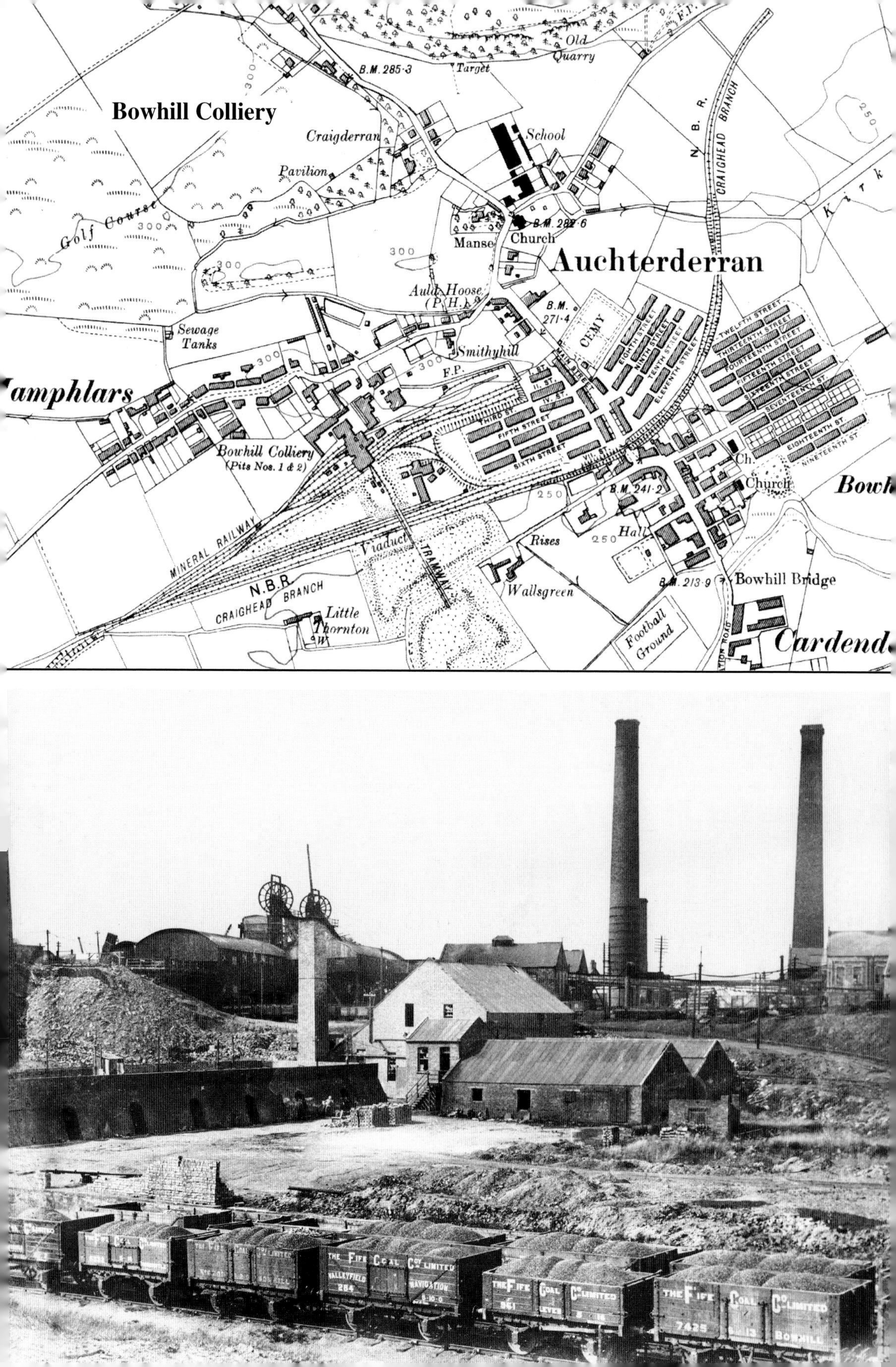

Bowhill Colliery
Old Quarry
B.M. 285·3
Target
Craigderran
School
N. B. R.
CRAIGHEAD BRANCH
Pavilion
Golf Course
300
250
B.M. 282·6
Manse
Church
Auchterderran
Auld Hoose (P. H.)
B.M. 271·4
CEMY
Sewage Tanks
Smithyhill
F.P.
MAIN STREET
EIGHTH STREET
NINTH STREET
TENTH STREET
ELEVENTH STREET
TWELFTH STREET
THIRTEENTH STREET
FOURTEENTH STREET
FIFTEENTH STREET
SIXTEENTH STREET
SEVENTEENTH ST.
EIGHTEENTH ST.
NINETEENTH ST.
THIRD ST.
FIFTH STREET
SIXTH STREET
amphlars
Bowhill Colliery (Pits Nos. 1 & 2)
Ch.
Church
B.M. 241·2
Bowh
MINERAL RAILWAY
Viaduct
TRAMWAY
Rises
Hall
N.B.R.
CRAIGHEAD BRANCH
Little Thornton
Wallsgreen
B.M. 213·9
Bowhill Bridge
Football Ground
Cardend
THE FIFE COAL Co LIMITED
VALLEYFIELD
NAVIGATION
BOWHILL

Branch to Engine Pit, Lady Helen Pit, West Pit

Engine Pit (Dundonald No. 3 Pit)

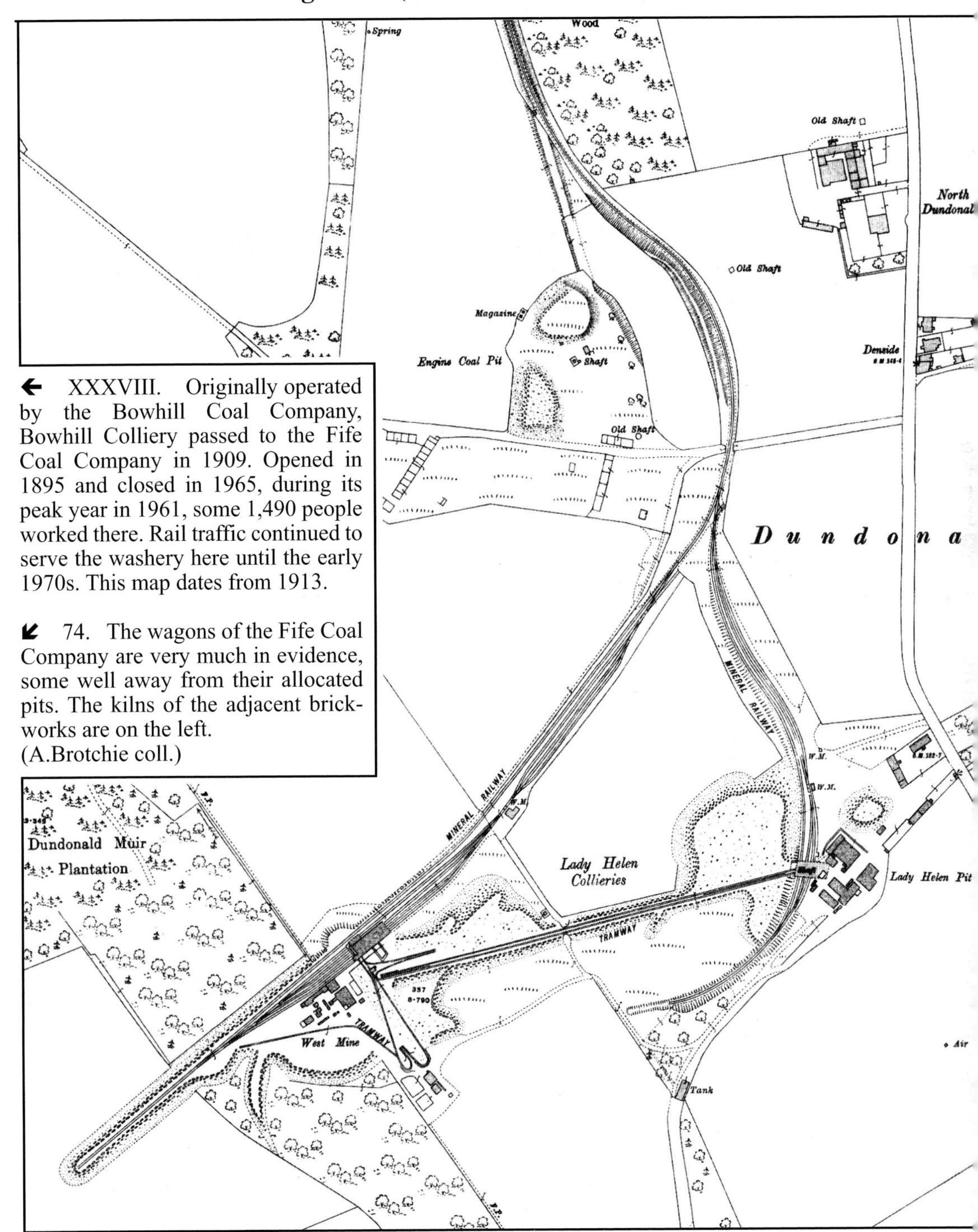

← XXXVIII. Originally operated by the Bowhill Coal Company, Bowhill Colliery passed to the Fife Coal Company in 1909. Opened in 1895 and closed in 1965, during its peak year in 1961, some 1,490 people worked there. Rail traffic continued to serve the washery here until the early 1970s. This map dates from 1913.

↙ 74. The wagons of the Fife Coal Company are very much in evidence, some well away from their allocated pits. The kilns of the adjacent brick-works are on the left. (A.Brotchie coll.)

XXXIX. This 1913 map shows the track into the pit removed and a new line bypassing the site, which opened in 1849, enroute to Lady Helen and West Pit.

Lady Helen Pit & West Pit (Dundonald Colliery)

75. The surface layout of Lady Helen Colliery (Dundonald) with a narrow-gauge railway leading to a trough. Sections of the trough wall are of brick construction.

Seen on the previous map, Lady Helen Pit was named after Viscountess Novar of Raith House, Kirkcaldy, and opened in around 1892. At its peak in 1957 it employed 455. Operated by the Dundonald Coal Co, it passed in 1910 to the Lochgelly Iron & Coal Company. The National Coal Board closed it in 1964.

Lady Helen Pit was initially sunk to a depth of 25 fathoms to the south of the Engine and Smithy pits of the old Dundonald Colliery.

West Pit (Dundonald No. 2), also known as Dothan Mine, was expanded in 1897 and closed in 1964. Two years previously it employed 250. In 1946 a new mine between Lady Helen and West Mine was proposed but was not developed. (National Mining Museum, Scotland)

Cardenden to Thornton Junction

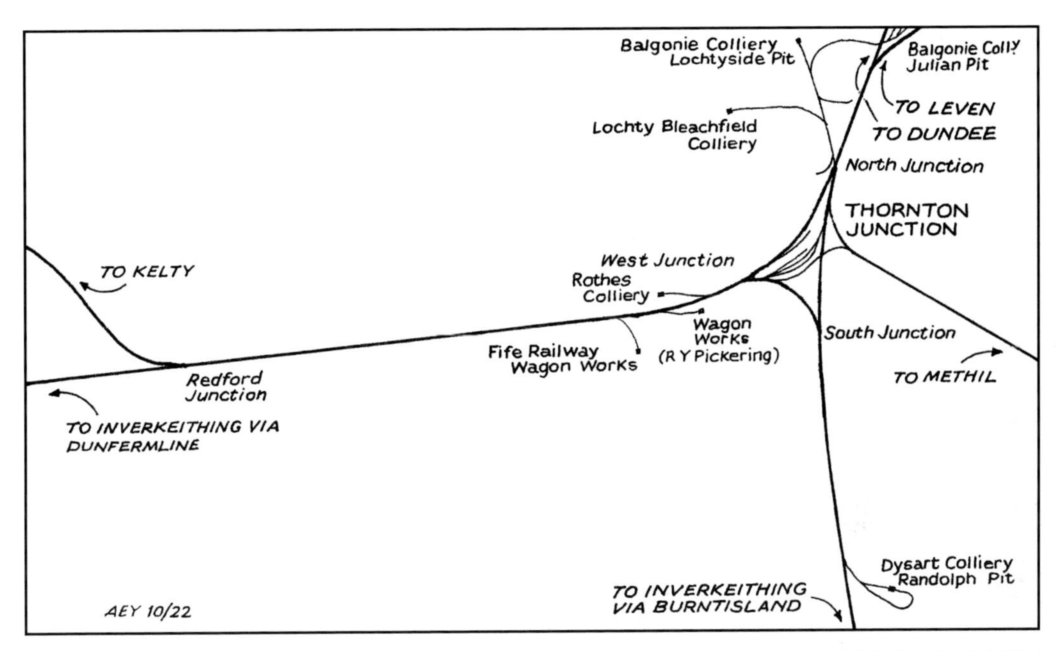

XL. The line in this section served fewer pits as it passed through Cardenden to Thornton Junction, which connected with the line from Inverkeithing to Dundee through Kirkcaldy. Thornton Junction became a major railway centre and a major employer, although its former station has now been replaced by the current Glenrothes with Thornton.
(A.E.Young)

Denend Colliery

XLI. The Denend Colliery was served by a tramway that connected with the Thornton line just west of Cardenden station. It was located at the north end of Carden Den with its two pits operated by the Denend Coal Company.

This 6in map, dated 1856, shows both the pit and the tramway which ran alongside the road before heading towards the pit head.

Closure appears to have taken place around 1895.

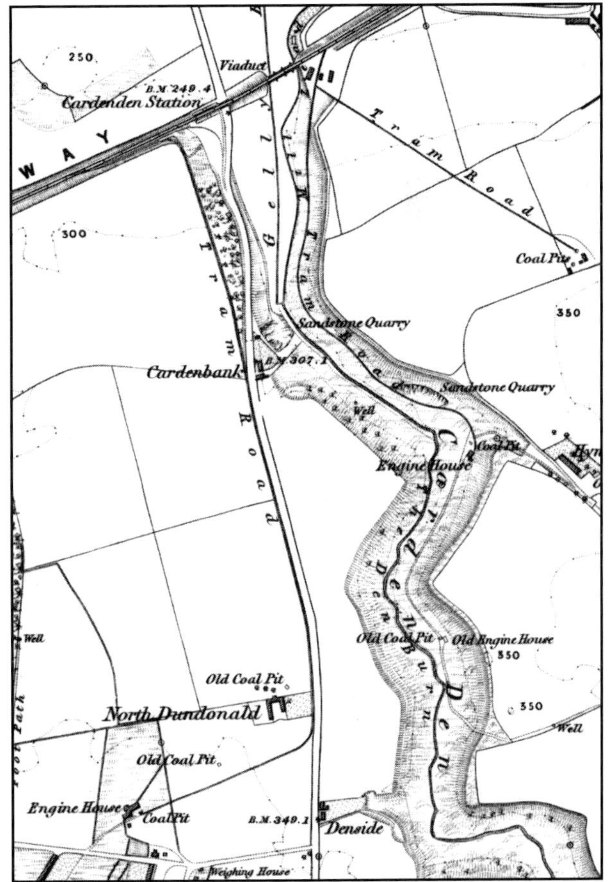

CARDENDEN

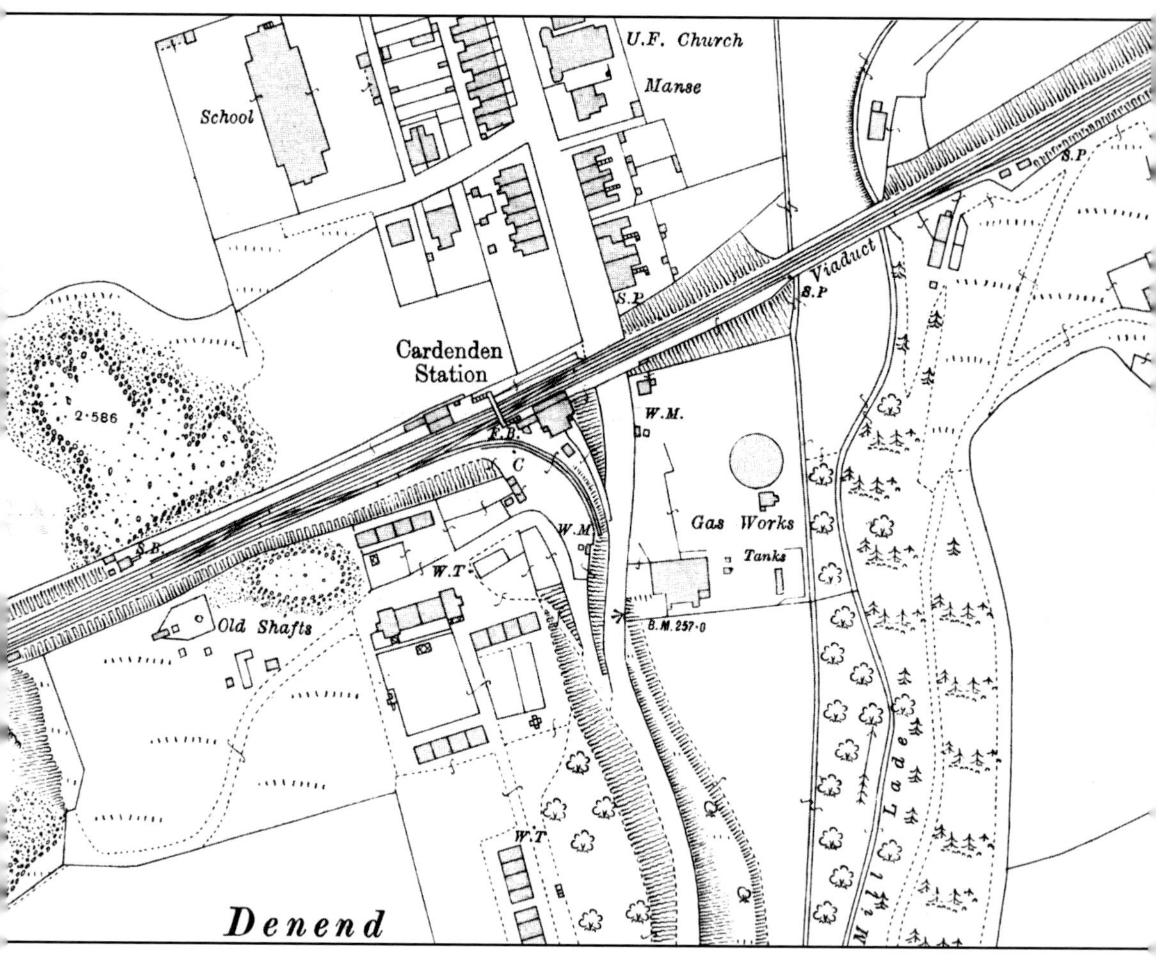

XLII. Opened on 4th September 1848 the station was renamed Cardenden for Bowhill in February 1908, before reverting to its previous name of Cardenden after 1956. The map dates from 1913.

Between the 1970s and 15th May 1989, Cardenden was the final calling point for most passenger trains (the section beyond Cardenden to Thornton Junction was used by only one passenger train during this period in order to keep the line open to passenger traffic). Lochgelly and Cardenden were used only during the morning and evening peaks during this period. From 15th May 1989 the line between Cardenden and Thornton Junction regained its passenger services and became part of the Fife Circle. The station lost its goods facilities on 29th March 1965.

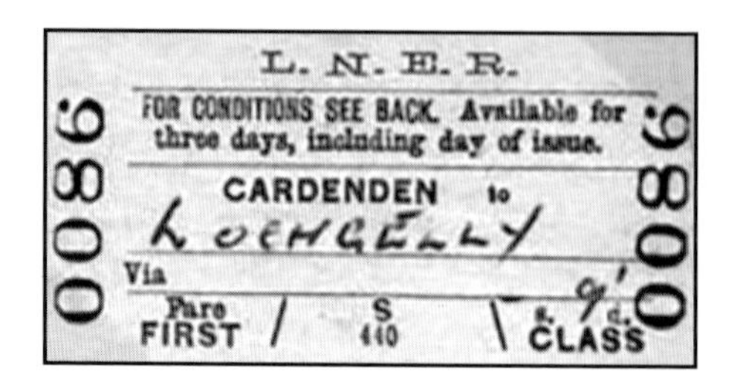

76. NBR 2-4-0 no. 391 calls with a train heading towards Cowdenbeath circa 1908. This locomotive was designed by Neilson in 1866. (J.Alsop coll.)

77. The station staff pose for the camera around 1906. (J.Alsop coll.)

78. The up platform with the station building is seen here on 9th August 1978 looking towards Cowdenbeath. The building has lost its distinctive wooden pattern having been covered in cladding. (A.E.Young)

79. This view, from 9th August 1978, looks towards Thornton Junction and shows the down platform shelter. (A.E.Young)

↓ 80. A similar view to that in picture 79 was taken on 1st August 2011 and shows the refurbished footbridge and replacement shelters, the main building having been demolished. (D.A.Lovett)

81. Looking towards Thornton on 1st August 2011 we see the more basic but practical platform shelter and extended platforms. (D.A.Lovett)

Cluny Colliery

XLIII. Opened in 1875 and closed in 1910 the site is shown on this 1913 map with its rail sidings still in place. Originally owned by the Bowhill Coal Company it later passed into the ownership of the Fife Coal Company.

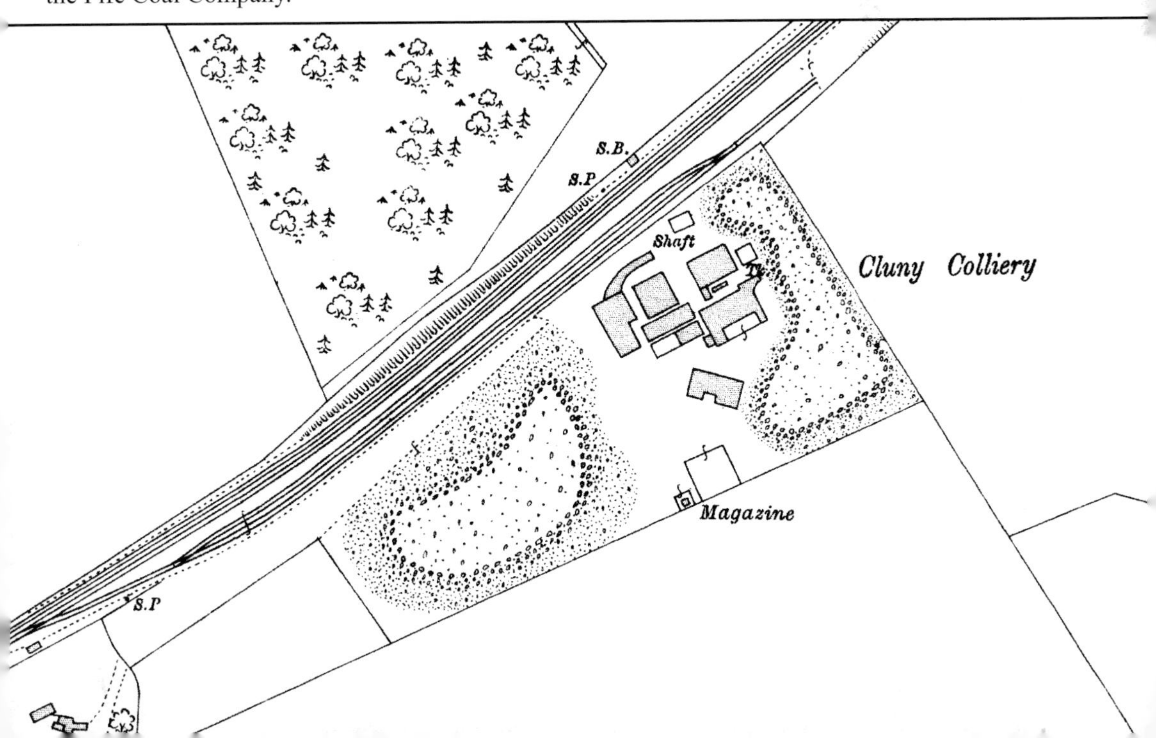

Clunie Lime Siding

82. Located on the south of the line, the siding was controlled by its own signal box which closed in 1928. The disused loading bank can be seen to the right of the road and to the left of the front of class 150 no. 150262, seen here in 1990 heading towards Cardenden. (W.Roberton)

Clunybridge Junction

XLIV. Seen here on this 1968 6in map, Clunybridge Junction gave access to Thornton Yard from the west.

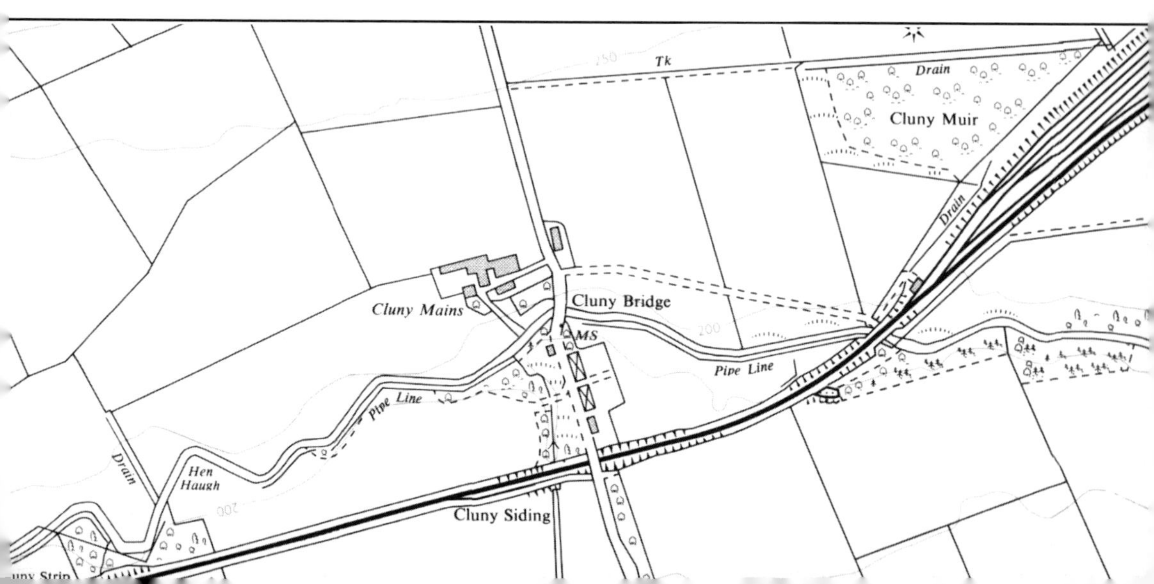

83. The line into Thornton Yard branches off just beyond the crossover. It is seen here in October 1989. (W.Roberton)

84. Carrying the first privatised ScotRail 'swoosh' livery class 158 no. 158728 heads towards Thornton Junction in 2004. (W.Roberton)

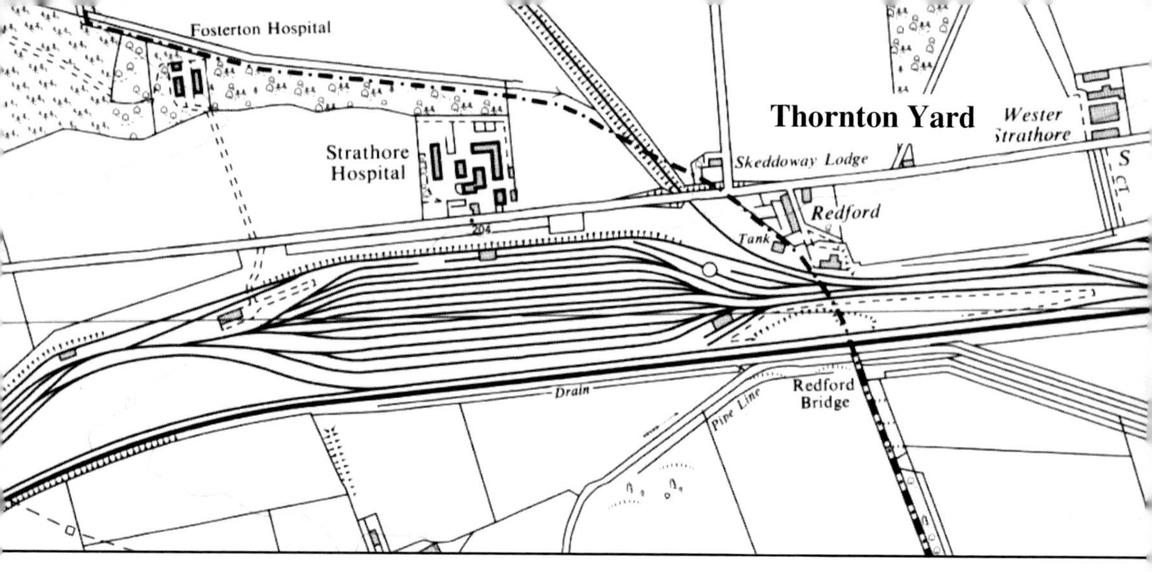

XLV. This 1966 6in to 1 mile map shows the yard that was developed following the publication of *The British Railways Modernisation Plan* in 1955. One of its aims was to rationalise the number of goods yards in areas and build new 'hump' shunting yards in several locations where there was a heavy concentration of freight traffic.

The Scottish Region was quick off the mark and Thornton was the first of the Modernisation Plan yards to open on 26th November 1956. It allowed most of the traffic from the Fife Coalfield to be collected and distributed from one of the 35 tracks and had the ability to handle 3,000 wagons each day. Located near to Rothes Colliery, the yard never reached its full potential due to the decline in coal mining and the switch to Merry Go Round (MGR) workings, which commenced in 1966. The yard was fitted with retarders to slow down wagons as they left the hump, allowing them to be shunted onto the various tracks in readiness for onward transit to their destination. Its decline continued with the last of the Fife pits closing in 2002 and open cast extraction following a decade later. The closure of the coal-fired power stations at Methil in 2000 (demolished 2011) and Longannet in 2016 (demolished 2019-21) heralded the end. Longannet at the time of its closure was the largest coal fired power station in Europe.

Speedlink traffic used the yard until its demise in 1991. For a time, it was used to store withdrawn rolling stock and, when this was cleared, much of the yard was abandoned. However, some road deliveries of open-cast mined coal continued to be loaded into MGR HAA hopper wagons for movement to Longannet Power Station until closure.

The site was abandoned and derelict but was part cleared to become a work site for supplies required for the reinstatement of the line from Thornton Junction to Levenmouth.

↙ 85. Several Mark 1 coaches, which were used on the dedicated Glasgow Central to Stranraer Harbour services for Sealink, are stored in the yard during 1985. Also in view are diesel locomotives nos 26021, 20220, 20227 and 20216. (W.Roberton)

86. By 1988, coal traffic was diminishing and the Speedlink wagon services were nearing an end resulting in plenty of siding space being available. (W.Roberton)

Rothes Colliery

XLVI. This 6in to 1 mile map is dated 1966, four years after the closure of Rothes Pit itself. This post-war colliery began production in 1957, although the sinking of the shafts commenced in 1946. It closed in 1962 and was abandoned in 1969. At its peak in 1960 it employed 1,235 people. It was Scotland's first super pit and was opened by Queen Elizabeth II on 30th June 1958. It was expected to employ round 2,000 miners and its reserves to last for 100 years. However, geological concerns and fear of flooding ensured that it was short-lived.

The establishing of the super pit resulted in the new town of Glenrothes, which was designated in 1948 under the New Towns Act 1946. It was built on land previously owned by the Earl of Rothes. However, the pit closure resulted in it having to diversify into other industries. The population in 2021 was just over 50,000.

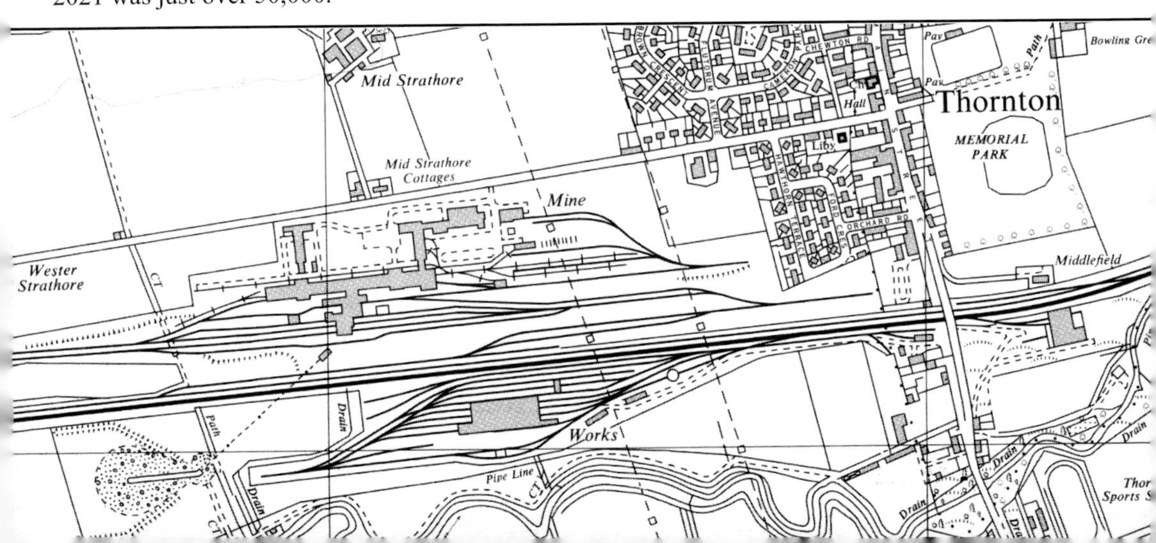

87. NCB Rothes no. 14, a Grant Ritchie 0-4-0ST built in 1901, is seen with its impressive spark arrestor fitted chimney on 26th May 1958. (Jim Peden/Industrial Railway Society)

88. The abandoned buildings at Rothes Pit are seen here in 1990. The track is part of the former 3ft narrow gauge system used for moving coal from the pit to the standard gauge tracks for loading and onward transit. The distinctive winding towers survived until demolished in 1993. (W.Roberton)

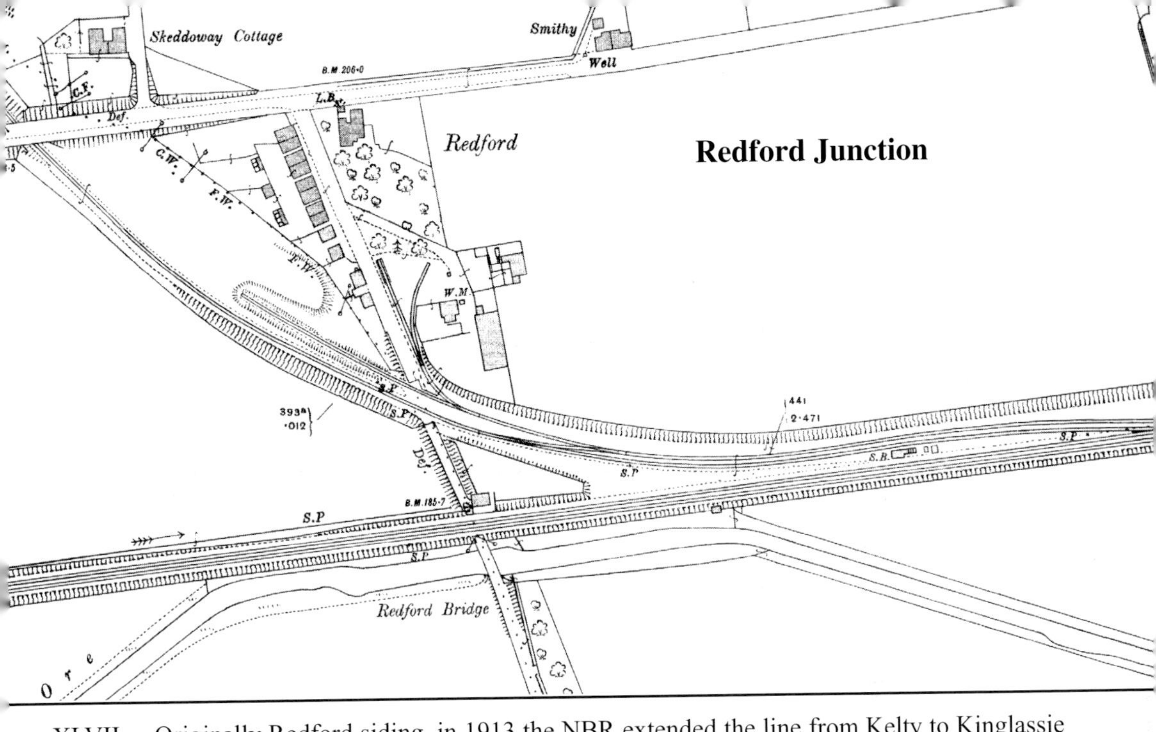

XLVII. Originally Redford siding, in 1913 the NBR extended the line from Kelty to Kinglassie Colliery to create a loop line. The map is dated that year.

The remnants of this line served Westfield Open Cast Colliery, which opened in 1956 on the site of the former Kirkness Colliery. Westfield closed initially in 1998 but was reactivated for a period from 2008 to clear remaining coal stocks. The remaining section of line was lifted in around 2014. The line from Kelty to Redford Junction will be covered in a future album.

89. Class 56 no. 56105 heads from Redford Junction towards Westfield Open Cast mine in 1997 with a rake of empty MGR wagons for loading. Thornton Yard diesel depot can be seen on the right. (W.Roberton)

Thornton Junction Traction Maintenance Depot (Third Shed)

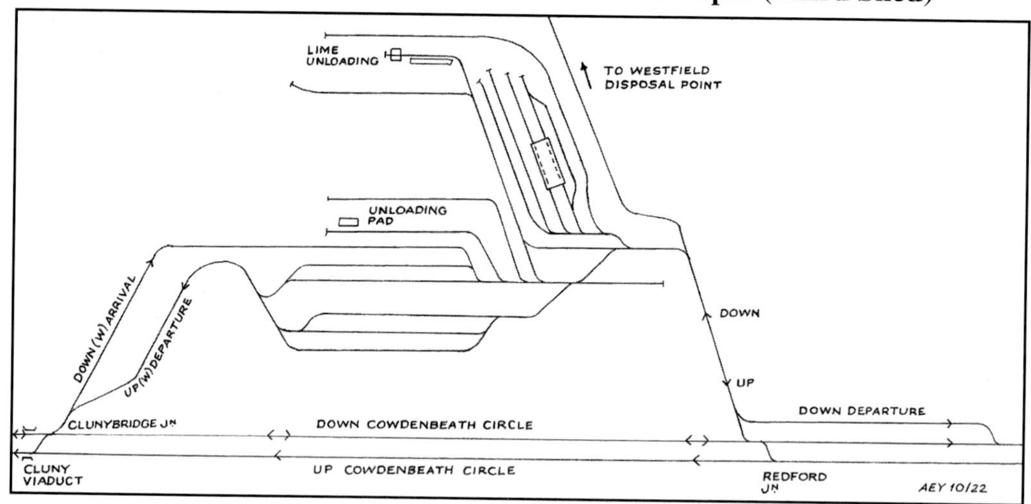

XLVIII. Thornton TMD and the remains of the yard are seen here in this 2008 track diagram. A new depot accessed from Thornton Yard was opened on 11th October 1984 and carried the depot code TJ (Thornton Junction) and replaced the facilities at Dunfermline Townhill. It was the third locomotive depot at Thornton, the previous two having been steam sheds.

DMUs for the Fife services were stabled and serviced overnight until the early 1980s, when the work was transferred to Haymarket Depot in Edinburgh.

The depot was closed by DB Schenker in 2010, although it remained in use as a base for John Cameron's steam locomotives no. 60009 *Union of South Africa* and no. 61994 *The Great Marquess* from 2007, until they moved away in 2013. The depot continued to be used by the support crew as an engineering store and for overnight accommodation when the locomotives were working locally. It was demolished in 2019. (A.E.Young)

90. The TMD was under construction when the 'Tay Forth Venturer' railtour took the Westfield branch on 16th June 1984. It opened four months later. (W.Roberton)

91. The newly completed shed is seen here in 1984 with two unidentified class 20 locomotives standing in the yard. The Westfield branch is on the left in this view. (W.Roberton)

92. Nos 61994 *The Great Marquess* & 60009 *Union of South Africa* are in their new shed on 14th April 2007.They had just arrived, having worked the 'Great Britain' from Inverness to Perth. (M.Mather)

93. LNER A4 class no. 60009 *Union of South Africa* and Deltic class 55 no. 55022 *Royal Scots Grey* stand outside the shed. The Deltic was at the shed as it was about to share the Alloa line reopening train with *The Great Marquess*, the two topping and tailing the special train. (M.Mather)

Thornton Shed (Second Shed)

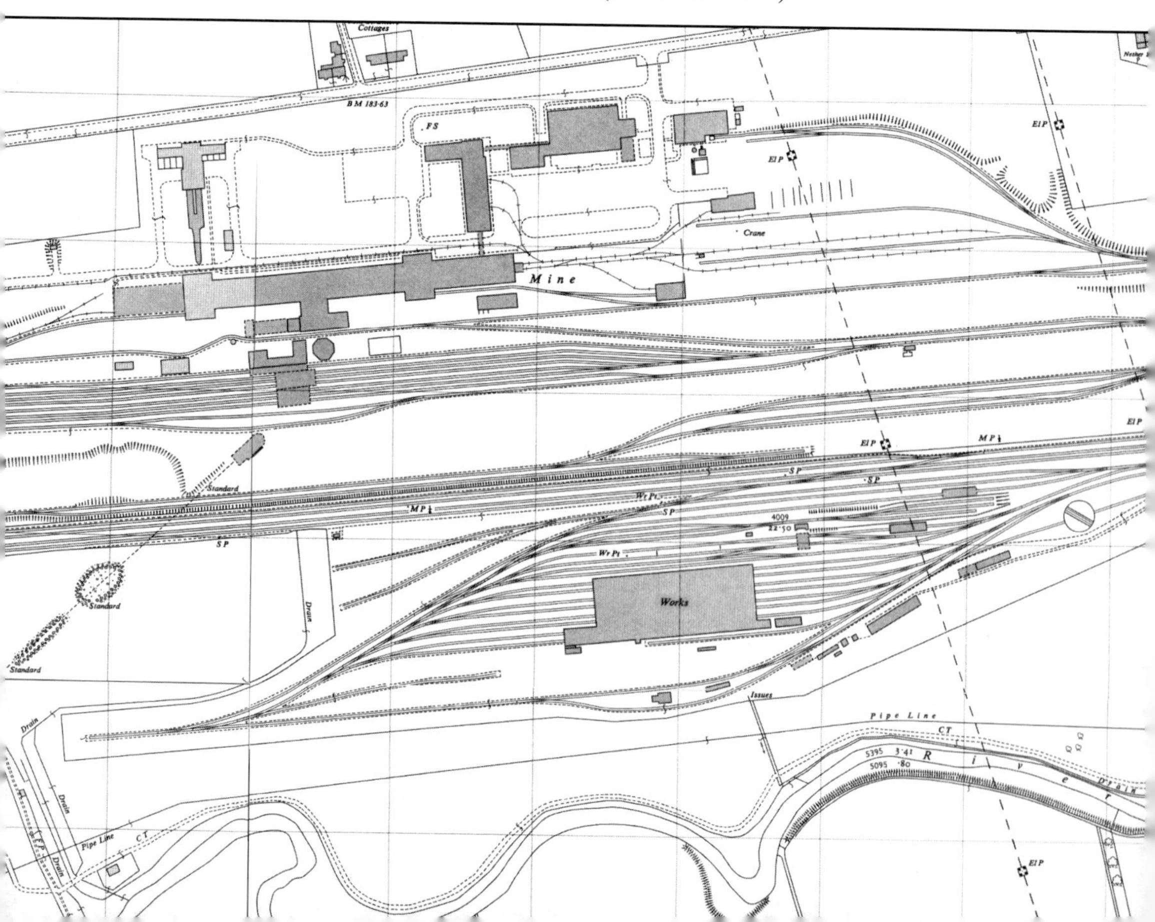

↙ XLIX. Authorised in 1931, the second shed opened on 20th July 1933 as a replacement for the earlier shed located closer to Thornton Junction station, which was suffering from mining subsidence and stood in the triangle of lines south of the station. It could accommodate 80 locos with provision for expansion if required. This 6in to 1 mile map is dated 1950.

In LNER days the initials THJ appeared on the buffer beams of the locomotives allocated to the shed. Following nationalisation in 1948, locomotives allocated to the shed carried 62A shed plates until it closed as a steam shed in April 1967, following the end of steam traction in the area.

It closed to diesel traction on 8th September 1969 with the shed building being demolished around 1970. The former shed site was used as an open-air stabling point. The depot lost its locomotive allocation in July 1970 when locomotives were reallocated to Dunfermline Townhill (DT).

94. Looking west from the top of the water tower, which can be seen on the left, the facilities look very new so we can ascertain that this was taken soon after opening in 1933. (A.Brotchie coll.)

95. Class D49/1 4-4-0 no. 62708 *Argyllshire*, J88 0-6-0T no. 68334, D30 4-4-0 no. 62418 *The Pirate* and K3 2-6-0 no. 61955 were in the shed yard on 8th June 1957. (G.W.Morrison)

96. The shed at Thornton Junction is seen here on 15th June 1961. Nearest the camera is LNER B1 class 4-6-0 no. 61343. (R.S.Carpenter)

97. Class J38 0-6-0 no. 65922 is in the shed yard in the Summer of 1966. It was withdrawn from Thornton in October of that year. (K.A.Gray/B.McCartney coll.)

Fife Railway Wagon Works

L. The Motherwell Wagon & Rolling Stock Co. provided a wagon repair facility known locally as the Fife Railway Wagon Works. The company was based at Flemington, Motherwell. The works was opened on 16th October 1906 by the firm of Shirlaw & Co. It was taken over by the Motherwell company in March 1908 although the business was continued under the Shirlaw Fenwick name for several years thereafter. The Motherwell company was placed in liquidation in January 1934 and its assets, including the Fife Railway Wagon Works, were sold off. This map is dated 1913.

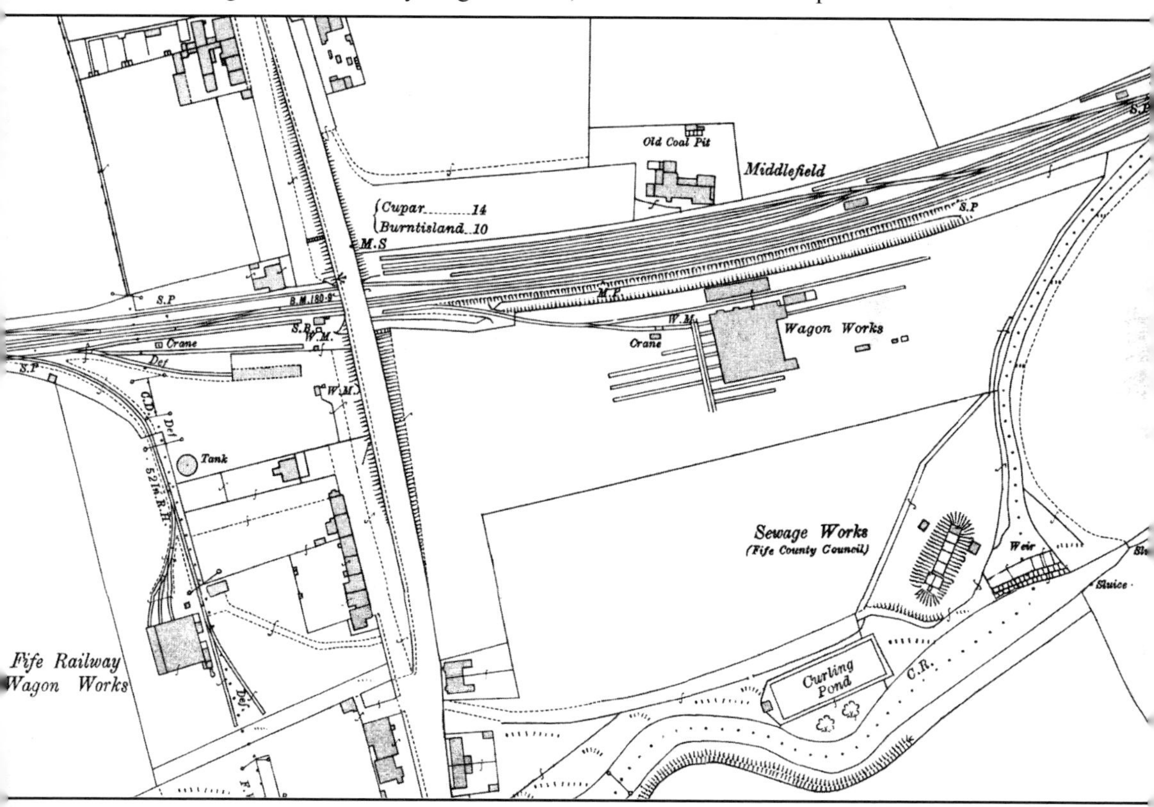

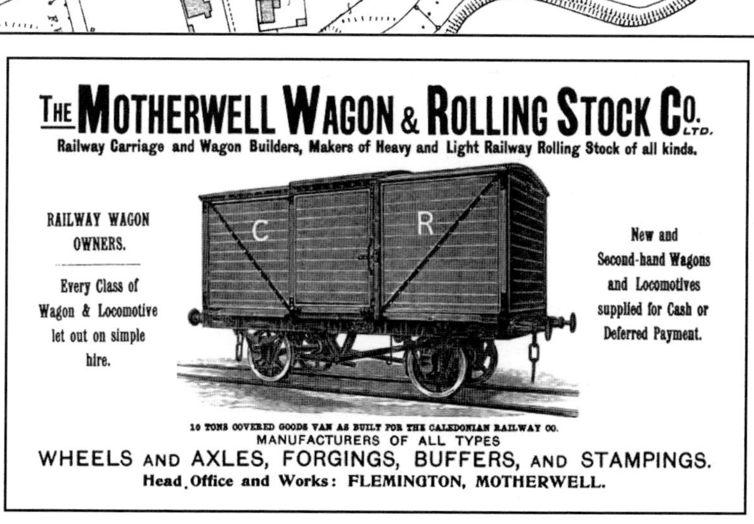

GLENROTHES WITH THORNTON

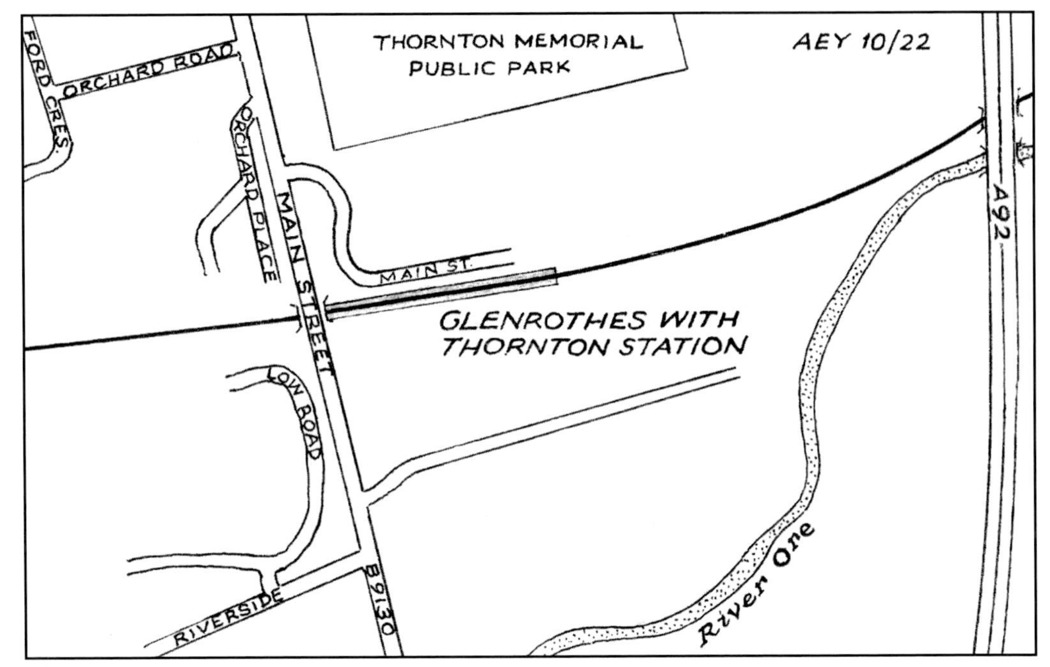

LI. Opened on 11th May 1992 to serve the Glenrothes and Thornton area, the station was located adjacent to the former Pickering Wagon Works with access off Main Street. The 1960 population of Glenrothes New Town was 8,100, which, by mid-2020, was over 38,000. The station is served by ScotRail Fife Circle services.

Although the station is actually in Thornton, it was named Glenrothes with Thornton, as its construction was part funded by Glenrothes Development Corporation. (A.E.Young)

98. Class 101 DMU no. 101691 passes the under-construction station in 1992. The building on the far left is the former Middlefield Engine House that once served a coal pit on the site. (W.Roberton)

99. The station car park has largely emptied during the early evening of 4th September 2014. (D.A.Lovett)

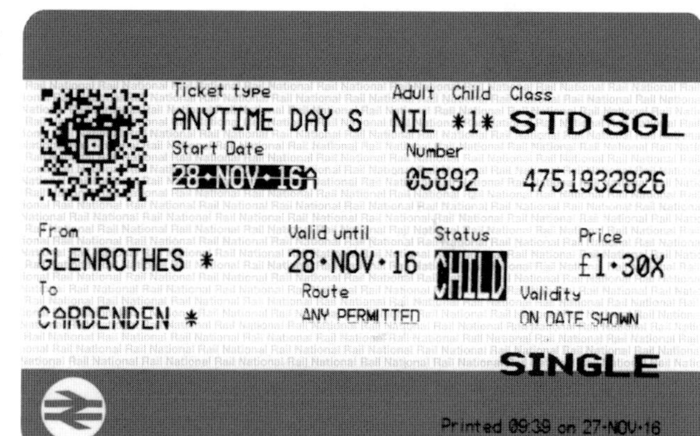

100. Looking towards Cowdenbeath, this view, taken on 4th September 2014, shows the access to the up platform via a pedestrian ramp. The down platform is accessed from the car park, although most trains use platform 1. (D.A.Lovett)

Pickering Wagon Works

A wagon works was opened by R.Y.Pickering & Co. Ltd in 1897 to repair wagons used to transport coal. Most were private owner wagons, which were produced in large numbers and carried the liveries of either collieries or coal merchants. With wagon bodies being wooden, damage could easily occur and most owners had repair contracts with companies to enable them to return to traffic as quickly as possible. The repair company was also responsible for the maintenance of wheels, brakes, buffers, couplings and frames. In 1939, when wartime regulations required all privately owned wagons to be used to best advantage under a 'Pooling' arrangement, there were some 36,710 in use. The wagon repair business of R.Y.Pickering & Co., along with the Thornton Works, was transferred to Wagon Repairs Ltd in 1923-24. The works can be seen in the centre of map L, after picture 97.

Originally from Yorkshire, John Pickering set up his works in Netherton, Wishaw, in 1864, his son Robert taking over the business in 1878. The company built and supplied new wagons, supplying railway companies with wagons by 1901 at the rate of some 3,000 a year. Wagons were also supplied to international operators, and customers included those in India, South America and South Africa.

Following reorganisation in 1911 the company was no longer Pickering owned. The name continued however and, following diversification in World War II, the company was still turning out over 50 wagons a week in 1950. A large contract for Pakistan Railways was completed in 1959, after which wagon building came to an end, BR workshops building most of their own wagons in-house.

The company again diversified into other areas of engineering and, despite a merger with Norbrit in 1966, the Norbrit – Pickering company in Wishaw was dissolved in 1987.

The wagon works at Thornton was still taking on apprentices in 1956 although we have been unable to ascertain an exact closure date. The site is now an industrial estate with some of the Pickering buildings being utilised for other purposes.

BRANCH WORKS

THORNTON, FIFE (N. B. Ry.)

RAWYARDS Near AIRDRIE (N. B. Ry.)

BEIGHTON Near SHEFFIELD (G. C. Ry.)

Established 1864.

R. Y. PICKERING & CO. LTD.

RAILWAY CARRIAGE AND WAGON BUILDERS
WHEEL MAKERS, ETC.

Chief Works and Offices WISHAW (Near GLASGOW) (C. Ry.)

Telegrams—"PICKERING, WISHAW." | Telephones—4 and 21 WISHAW.

London Office: 3 VICTORIA STREET, WESTMINSTER, S.W.

Railway Wagons built to Customers' own requirements, and Wagons repaired, converted, and re-constructed.
Hutches and Colliery Furnishings of all descriptions.
Wagon Castings, Brasses, Self-contained Buffers, Wagon Oak and all classes of mountings supplied.

REPAIRING STATIONS

DUNDEE PERTH
EDINBURGH
STIRLING OMOA
HAMILTON (Ross and Strathaven Junctions)
MOTHERWELL

And Various Stations in ENGLAND

➚ *(top)* 101. Class 150 no. 150262 in Regional Railways livery calls at Glenrothes with Thornton in 1992. In the background are some of the former Pickering buildings now in industrial use. (W.Roberton)

➚ *(centre)* 102. The former Pickering Wagon Works buildings are in industrial use on 29th April 2013. (W.Roberton)

Thornton West Junction

➔ 103. Class 26 no. 26029 hauls a coal train past Thornton West Junction, the sign being to the right of the locomotive. The remains of Rothes Colliery is in the background on 22nd June 1982. (T.Heavyside)

Edinburgh
150262
Way out
Glenrothes
HELL
HOMES
LIMITED
THOMAS
MITCHELL
HOMES
LIMITED

Thornton Junction (First Shed)

LII. Limited facilities were provided at Thornton for two locomotives working the Anstruther branch by 1880. There was a coaling stage, turntable and two sidings. No pits were provided,

Thornton's first shed opened in 1894. It had four covered roads and could accommodate 16 locomotives under cover. Located in the triangle close to the station it had little room for expansion, which was required due to the large amount of coal traffic. Like the nearby station, the locomotive shed was also suffering from subsidence caused by local mining, a problem for heavy locomotives requiring coaling and maintenance. The first shed closed in 1933 upon the opening of the second shed (see pictures 94 to 97). This was the layout in 1913.

➔ 104. The first shed is seen here during NBR days. It closed in 1933 and was replaced by a new shed on the Cowdenbeath line. (A.Brotchie)

THORNTON JUNCTION

105. Seen here in 1913, the station was originally built of sandstone on the downside but was soon replaced by a central island platform. Access from the village was by a footbridge at the northern end of the station, which also carried a right of way, being some 120ft long crossing all lines. The station had an island platform with single track bay platforms in the centre. These were either side of the main building, constructed in 1885, with generous facilities that were required by passengers changing trains from one line to another, including substantial canopies. A separate platform for the Buckhaven line services to Methil was built on the eastern side and was served by the footbridge at the northern end of the station. The northern bay was used by trains to and from Leven, Anstruther and St. Andrews, and the southern one originally for terminating trains from the Dunfermline and Methil lines.

Subsidence from the mining industry resulted in the station being rebuilt in the early 1930s, the original buildings being demolished. The replacements, including the platforms, were rebuilt in timber, enabling them to be repaired quickly following further subsidence. This was done on several occasions.

When the Leven line closed to passengers on 6th October 1969, its role as a junction station was no more. It closed too and was subsequently demolished. Goods facilities had been withdrawn on 26th April 1965, although the nearby yard remained open for marshalling coal trains. (R.S.Carpenter coll.)

106. An Edwardian postcard view of the station taken in around 1910. The station has not yet suffered subsidence issues. (J.Alsop coll.)

107. The large island platform dominates this view with the single line bay platform accessible from both the main platforms. This would have been used by the branch line train serving the lines into East Fife. (W.Lynn)

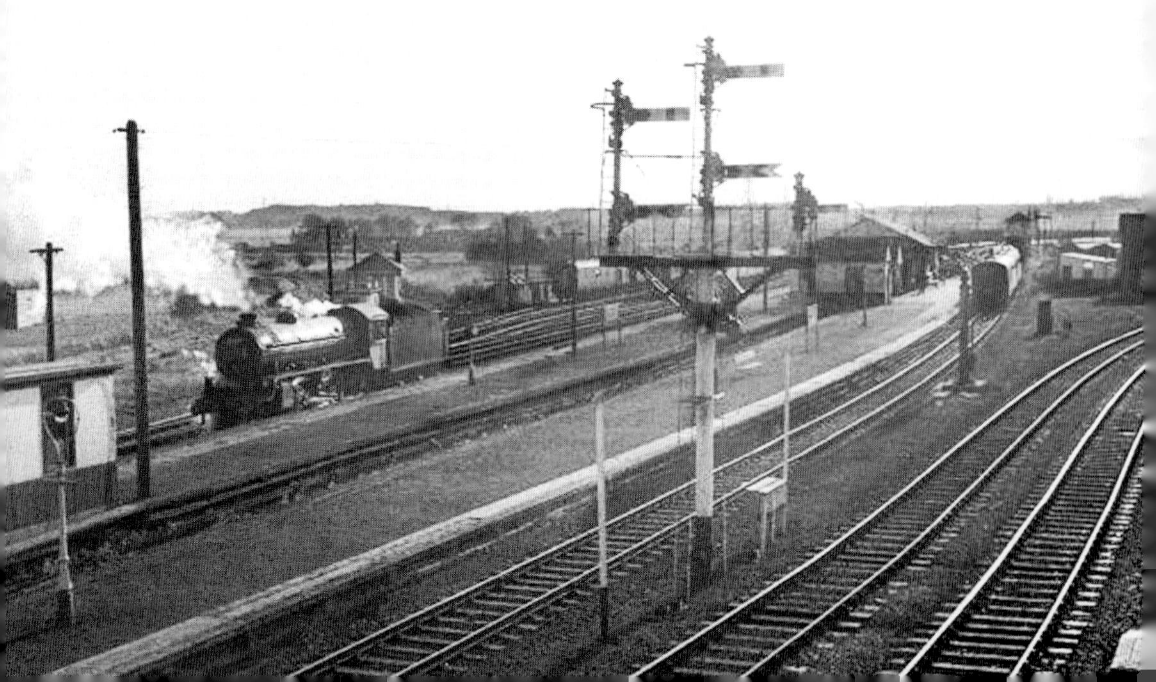

108. Looking south west from the platform around 1950. LNER class B1 4-6-0 no. 61147 is on a Dundee to Edinburgh service. D29 class 4-4-0 no. 62412 *Dirk Hatteraick* waits in the bay platform ready to work a Thornton – Fife coast service. Note the packing work under the platforms to try and keep them level; a result of subsidence from nearby coal mining activity. (W.A.Camwell/ Stephenson Locomotive Society)

109. Class D34 4-4-0 no. 62478 *Glen Quoich* waits in the south end bay platform on 21st August 1959. The timber platform decking is very evident in this picture. (A.G.Forsyth/ Initial Photographics)

110. WD 2-8-0 no. 90628 passes Thornton Station signal box on 30th September 1965. The box opened on 28th April 1878 and closed on 25th March 1973. (J.F.Aylard/ Initial Photographics)

3. Cowdenbeath South Junction to Lumphinnans Central Junction via Cowdenbeath New

COWDENBEATH NEW

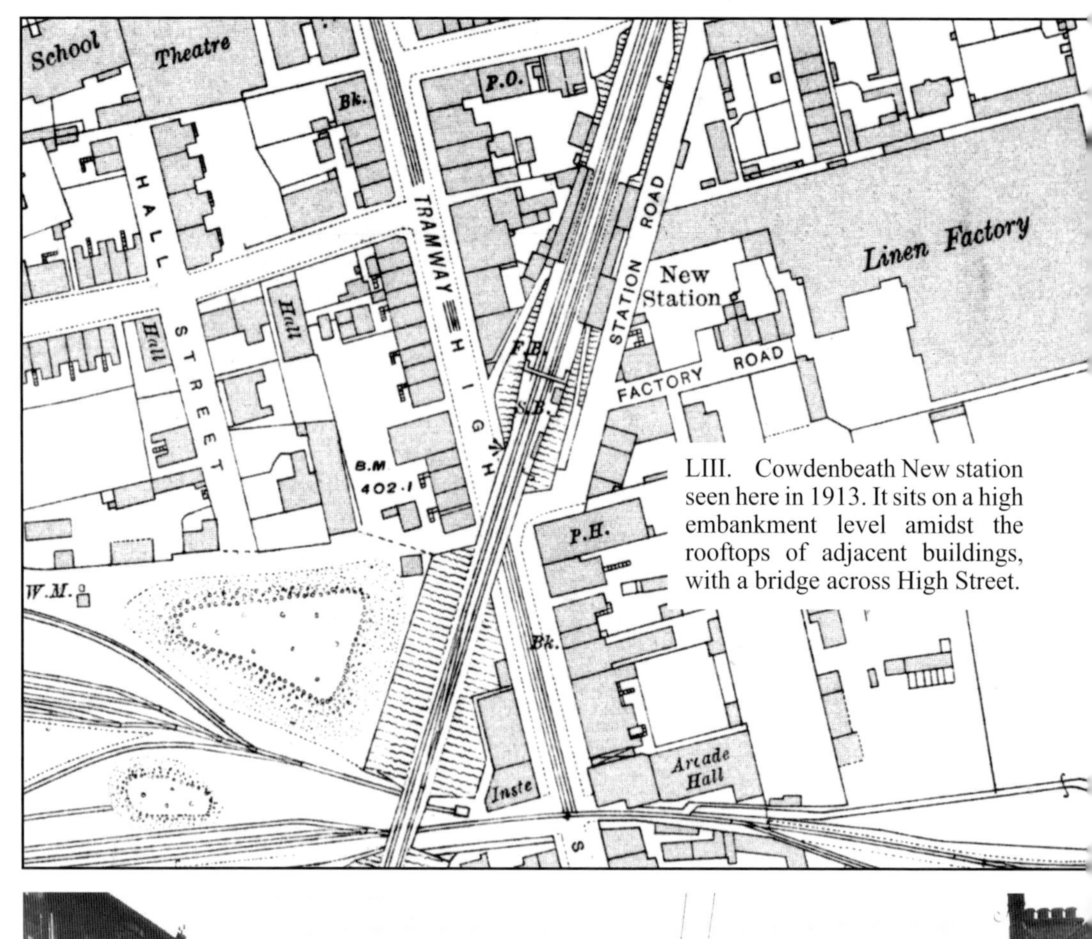

LIII. Cowdenbeath New station seen here in 1913. It sits on a high embankment level amidst the rooftops of adjacent buildings, with a bridge across High Street.

↙ 111. Looking towards the station down the High Street, a tram of the Dunfermline & District Tramway Company heads north towards Kelty or Lochgelly and is about to cross over the Fife Coal Company's level crossing. The 3ft 6in tramway ran from Rosyth in the west as far as Lochgelly between 1909 and closure in 1937. The former tram depot in Cowdenbeath became a bus depot. (Cowdenbeath Library)

112. The refurbished bridge over High Street is seen here on 7th February 2022, with the junction for Station Road to the left of the public house. (W.Roberton)

113. This picture dates from August 1914 and shows the main station building on the right as a train enters the platform heading towards Dunfermline. (J.Alsop coll.)

114. We are looking towards Dunfermline following the rebuilding of the station buildings on 4th September 1965. The signal box opened in 1901 and closed in 1981 when control of the lines passed to Edinburgh Signalling Centre. (H.Stevenson)

2483
| 12 | 11 | 10 | 9 | 8 | 7 |
BRITISH RAILWAYS (H
COWDENBEATH (NEW)
PLATFORM TICKET 1d
Available ONE HOUR on Day of issue only
NOT VALID IN TRAINS. NOT TRANSFERABLE
To be given up when leaving Platform
FOR CONDITIONS SEE BACK
| 1 | 2 | 3 | 4 | 5 | 6 |
2483

115. Class 40 no. D222 *Laconia* pauses with the 14.55 Perth to Edinburgh service on 4th September 1965. The train had travelled over the Glenfarg line via Bridge of Earn and Kinross Junction. (H.Stevenson)

116. Class 20 no. 20222 heads south from Cowdenbeath with an MGR coal train on 22nd June 1982. A pair of class 20s (nos 20206 and 20226) are on the rear of the train. This form of operation was a regular feature of the MGR trains to Longannet, facilitating the speedy reversals necessary on some routings. (T.Heavyside)

117. The main station building is on the up platform. It dates from the early 1960s and is seen here on 14th April 2011. (D.A.Lovett)

118. This view finds us looking towards Thornton Junction from the footbridge on 14th April 2011. (D.A.Lovett)

119. Class 170 no. 170461, carrying First ScotRail livery, pauses at platform 2 with a Fife Circle train for Edinburgh via Dunfermline on 14th April 2011. (D.A.Lovett)

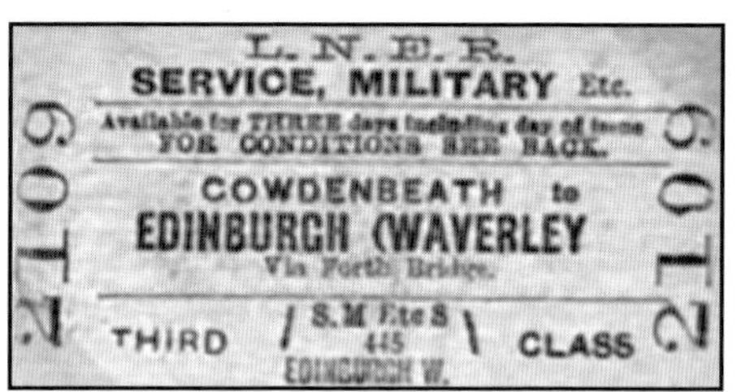

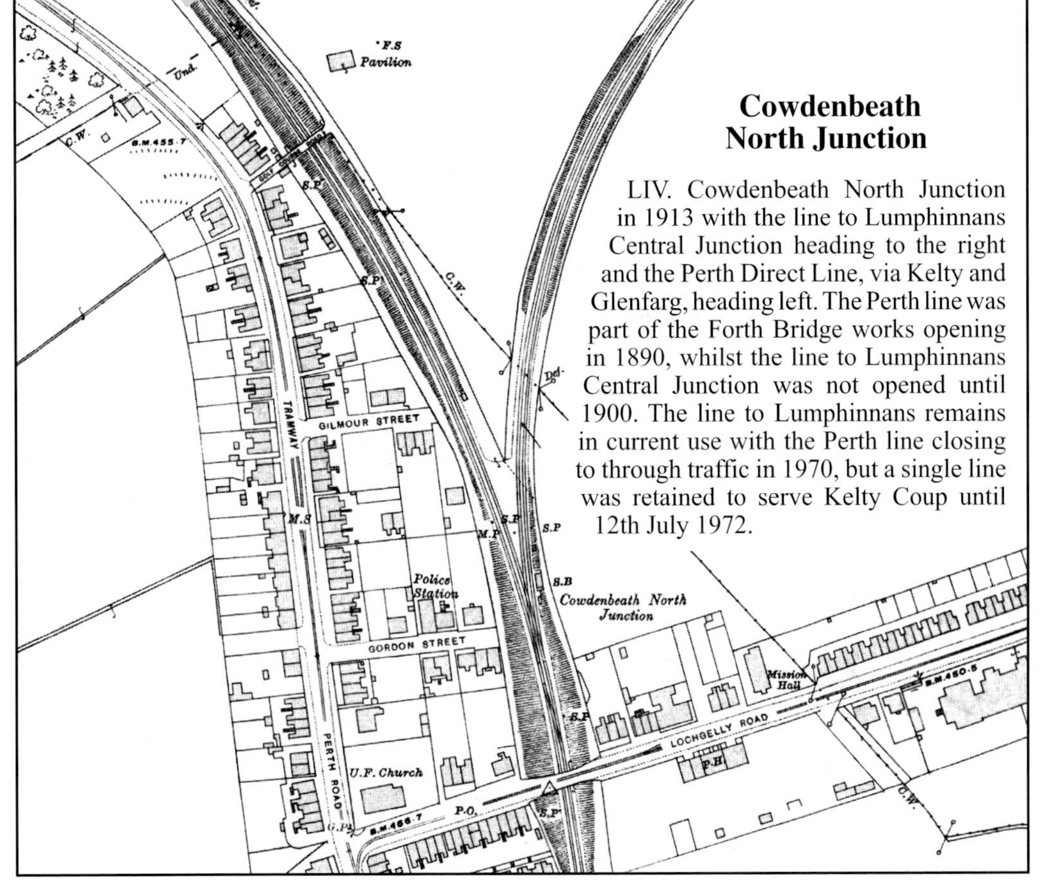

Cowdenbeath North Junction

LIV. Cowdenbeath North Junction in 1913 with the line to Lumphinnans Central Junction heading to the right and the Perth Direct Line, via Kelty and Glenfarg, heading left. The Perth line was part of the Forth Bridge works opening in 1890, whilst the line to Lumphinnans Central Junction was not opened until 1900. The line to Lumphinnans remains in current use with the Perth line closing to through traffic in 1970, but a single line was retained to serve Kelty Coup until 12th July 1972.

120. Former War Department 2-8-0 no. 90020 leaves the line from Lumphinnans Central Junction at Cowdenbeath North Junction, heading south with a coal train on 30th September 1965. The line on the left is the Perth Direct line opened in 1890. (J.F.Aylard/Initial Photographics)

EVOLVING THE
Vic Mitchell and Keith Smith
ULTIMATE RAIL ENCYCLOPEDIA
INTERNATIONAL

126a Camelsdale Road, GU27 3RJ. Tel:01730 813169
A-978 0 906520 B- 978 1 873793 C- 978 1 901706 D-978 1 904474
E - 978 1 906008 F - 978 1 908174 G - 978 1 910356

Our RAILWAY titles are listed below. Please check availability by looking at our website **www.middletonpress.co.uk,** telephoning us or by requesting a Brochure which includes our LATEST RAILWAY TITLES also our TRAMWAY, TROLLEYBUS, MILITARY and COASTAL series.

email:info@middletonpress.co.uk

A
Abergavenny to Merthyr C 91 8
Abertillery & Ebbw Vale Lines D 84 5
Aberystwyth to Carmarthen E 90 1
Alnmouth to Berwick G 50 0
Alton - Branch Lines to A 11 6
Ambergate to Buxton G 28 9
Ambergate to Mansfield G 39 5
Andover to Southampton A 82 6
Ascot - Branch Lines around A 64 2
Ashburton - Branch Line to B 95 4
Ashford - Steam to Eurostar B 67 1
Ashford to Dover A 48 2
Austrian Narrow Gauge D 04 3
Avonmouth - BL around D 42 5
Aylesbury to Rugby D 91 3

B
Baker Street to Uxbridge D 90 6
Bala to Llandudno E 87 1
Banbury to Birmingham D 27 2
Banbury to Cheltenham E 63 5
Bangor to Holyhead F 01 7
Bangor to Portmadoc E 72 7
Barking to Southend C 80 2
Barmouth to Pwllheli E 53 6
Barry - Branch Lines around D 50 0
Bartlow - Branch Lines to F 27 7
Basingstoke to Salisbury A 89 4
Bath Green Park to Bristol C 36 9
Bath to Evercreech Junction A 60 4
Beamish 40 years on rails E94 9
Bedford to Wellingborough D 31 9
Berwick to Drem F 64 2
Berwick to St. Boswells F 75 8
B'ham to Tamworth & Nuneaton F 63 5
Birkenhead to West Kirby F 61 1
Birmingham to Wolverhampton E253
Blackburn to Hellifield F 95 6
Bletchley to Cambridge D 94 4
Bletchley to Rugby E 07 9
Bodmin - Branch Lines around B 83 1
Bolton to Preston G 61 6
Boston to Lincoln F 80 2
Bournemouth to Evercreech Jn A 46 8
Bradshaw's History F18 5
Bradshaw's Rail Times 1850 F 13 0
Branch Lines series - see town names
Brecon to Neath D 43 2
Brecon to Newport D 16 6
Brecon to Newtown E 06 2
Brighton to Eastbourne A 16 1
Brighton to Worthing A 03 1
Bristol to Taunton D 03 6
Bromley South to Rochester B 23 7
Bromsgrove to Birmingham D 87 6
Bromsgrove to Gloucester D 73 9
Broxbourne to Cambridge F16 1
Brunel - A railtour D 74 6
Bude - Branch Line to B 29 9
Burnham to Evercreech Jn B 68 0
Buxton to Stockport G 32 6

C
Cambridge to Ely D 55 5
Canterbury - BLs around B 58 9
Cardiff to Dowlais (Cae Harris) E 47 5
Cardiff to Pontypridd E 95 6
Cardiff to Swansea E 42 0
Carlisle to Beattock G 69 2
Carlisle to Hawick E 85 7
Carmarthen to Fishguard E 66 6
Caterham & Tattenham Corner B251
Central & Southern Spain NG E 91 8
Chard and Yeovil - BLs a C 30 7
Charing Cross to Orpington A 96 3
Cheddar - Branch Line to B 90 9
Cheltenham to Andover C 43 7
Cheltenham to Redditch D 81 4
Chesterfield to Lincoln G 21 0
Chester to Birkenhead F 21 5
Chester to Manchester F 51 2
Chester to Rhyl E 93 2
Chester to Warrington F 40 6
Chichester to Portsmouth A 14 7
Clacton and Walton - BLs to F 04 8
Clapham Jn to Beckenham Jn B 36 7
Cleobury Mortimer - BLs a E 18 5
Clevedon & Portishead - BLs to D180
Consett to South Shields E 57 4
Cornwall Narrow Gauge D 56 2
Corris and Vale of Rheidol E 65 9
Coventry to Leicester G 00 5
Craven Arms to Llandeilo E 35 2
Craven Arms to Wellington E 33 8
Crawley to Littlehampton A 34 5
Crewe to Manchester F 57 4
Crewe to Wigan G 12 8
Cromer - Branch Lines around C 26 0
Cromford and High Peak G 35 7
Croydon to East Grinstead B 48 0
Crystal Palace & Catford Loop B 87 1
Cyprus Narrow Gauge E 13 0

D
Darjeeling Revisited F 09 3
Darlington Leamside Newcastle E 28 4
Darlington to Newcastle D 98 2
Dartford to Sittingbourne B 34 3
Denbigh - Branch Lines around F 32 1
Derby to Chesterfield G 11 1
Derby to Nottingham G 45 6
Derby to Stoke-on-Trent F 93 2
Derwent Valley - BL to the D 06 7
Devon Narrow Gauge E 09 3
Didcot to Banbury D 02 9
Didcot to Swindon C 84 0
Didcot to Winchester C 13 0
Diss to Norwich G 22 7
Dorset & Somerset NG D 76 0
Douglas - Laxey - Ramsey E 75 8
Douglas to Peel C 88 8
Douglas to Port Erin C 55 0
Douglas to Ramsey D 39 5
Dover to Ramsgate A 78 9
Drem to Edinburgh G 06 7
Dublin Northwards in 1950s E 31 4
Dunstable - Branch Lines to E 27 7

E
Ealing to Slough C 42 0
Eastbourne to Hastings A 27 7
East Croydon to Three Bridges A 53 6
Eastern Spain Narrow Gauge E 56 7
East Grinstead - BLs to A 07 9
East Kent Light Railway A 61 1
East London - Branch Lines of C 44 4
East London Line B 80 0
East of Norwich - Branch Lines E 69 7
Effingham Junction - BLs a A 74 1
Ely to Norwich C 90 1
Enfield Town & Palace Gates D 32 6
Epsom to Horsham A 30 7
Eritrean Narrow Gauge E 38 3
Euston to Harrow & Wealdstone C 89 5
Exeter to Barnstaple B 15 2
Exeter to Newton Abbot C 49 9
Exeter to Tavistock B 69 5
Exmouth - Branch Lines to B 00 8

F
Fairford - Branch Line to A 52 9
Falmouth, Helston & St. Ives C 74 1
Fareham to Salisbury A 67 3
Faversham to Dover B 05 3
Felixstowe & Aldeburgh - BL to D 20 3
Fenchurch Street to Barking C 20 8
Festiniog - 50 yrs of enterprise C 83 3
Festiniog 1946-55 E 01 7
Festiniog in the Fifties B 68 8
Festiniog in the Sixties B 91 6
Ffestiniog in Colour 1955-82 F 25 3
Finsbury Park to Alexandra Pal C 02 8
French Metre Gauge Survivors F 88 8
Frome to Bristol B 77 0

G
Gainsborough to Sheffield G 17 3
Galashiels to Edinburgh F 52 9
Gloucester to Bristol D 35 7
Gloucester to Cardiff D 66 1
Gosport - Branch Lines around A 36 9
Greece Narrow Gauge D 72 2
Guildford to Redhill A 63 5

H
Hampshire Narrow Gauge D 36 4
Harrow to Watford D 14 2
Harwich & Hadleigh - BLs to F 02 4
Harz Revisited F 62 8
Hastings to Ashford A 37 6
Hawick to Galashiels F 36 9
Hawkhurst - Branch Line to A 66 6
Hayling - Branch Line to A 12 3
Hay-on-Wye - BL around D 92 0
Haywards Heath to Seaford A 28 4
Hemel Hempstead - BLs to D 88 3
Henley, Windsor & Marlow - BLa C77 2
Hereford to Newport D 54 8
Hertford & Hatfield - BLs a E 58 1
Hertford Loop E 71 0
Hexham to Carlisle D 75 3
Hexham to Hawick F 08 6
Hitchin to Peterborough D 07 4
Horsham - Branch Lines to A 02 4
Hull, Hornsea and Withernsea G 27 2
Hull to Scarborough G 60 9
Huntingdon - Branch Line to A 93 2

I
Ilford to Shenfield C 97 0
Ilfracombe - Branch Line to B 21 3
Ilkeston to Chesterfield G 26 5
Inverkeithing to Thornton Jct G 76 0
Ipswich to Diss F 81 9
Ipswich to Saxmundham C 41 3
Isle of Man Railway Journey F 94 9
Isle of Wight Lines - 50 yrs C 12 3
Italy Narrow Gauge F 17 8

K
Kent Narrow Gauge C 45 1
Kettering to Nottingham F 82-6
Kidderminster to Shrewsbury E 10 9
Kingsbridge - Branch Line to C 98 7
Kings Cross to Potters Bar E 62 8
King's Lynn to Hunstanton F 58 1
Kingston & Hounslow Loops A 83 3
Kingswear - Branch Line to C 17 8

L
Lambourn - Branch Line to C 70 3
Launceston & Princetown - BLs C 19 2
Leeds to Selby G 47 0
Leek - Branch Line From G 01 2
Leicester to Burton F 85 7
Leicester to Nottingham G 15 9
Lewisham to Dartford A 92 5
Lincoln to Cleethorpes F 56 7
Lincoln to Doncaster G 03 6
Lines around Newmarket G 54 8
Lines around Stamford F 98 7
Lines around Wimbledon B 75 6
Lines North of Stoke G 29 6
Liverpool to Runcorn G 72 2
Liverpool Street to Chingford D 01 2
Liverpool Street to Ilford C 34 5
Llandeilo to Swansea E 46 8
London Bridge to Addiscombe B 20 6
London Bridge to East Croydon A 58 1
Longmoor - Branch Lines to A 41 3
Looe - Branch Line to C 22 2
Loughborough to Ilkeston G 24 1
Loughborough to Nottingham F 68 0
Lowestoft - BLs around E 40 6
Ludlow to Hereford E 14 7
Lydney - Branch Lines around E 26 0
Lyme Regis - Branch Line to A 45 1
Lynton - Branch Line to B 04 6

M
Machynlleth to Barmouth E 54 3
Maesteg and Tondu Lines F 06 2
Majorca & Corsica Narrow Gauge F 41 3
Manchester to Bacup G 46 3
Mansfield to Doncaster G 23 4
March - Branch Lines around B 09 1
Market Drayton - BLs around F 67 3
Market Harborough to Newark F 86 4
Marylebone to Rickmansworth D 49 4
Melton Constable to Yarmouth Bch E031
Midhurst - Branch Lines of E 78 9
Midhurst - Branch Lines to F 00 0
Minehead - Branch Line to A 80 2
Monmouth - Branch Lines to E 20 8
Monmouthshire Eastern Valleys D 71 5
Moretonhampstead - BL to C 27 7
Moreton-in-Marsh to Worcester D 26 5
Morpeth to Bellingham F 87 1
Mountain Ash to Neath D 80 7

N
Newark to Doncaster F 78 9
Newbury to Westbury C 66 6
Newcastle to Alnmouth G 36 4
Newcastle to Hexham D 69 2
Newmarket to Haughley & Laxfield G 71 5
New Mills to Sheffield G 44 9
Newport (IOW) - Branch Lines to A 26 0
Newquay - Branch Lines to C 71 0
Newton Abbot to Plymouth C 60 4
Newtown to Aberystwyth E 41 3
Northampton to Peterborough F 92 5
North East German NG D 44 9
Northern Alpine Narrow Gauge F 37 6
Northern Spain Narrow Gauge E 83 3
North London Line B 94 7
North of Birmingham F 55 0
North of Grimsby - Branch Lines G 09 8
North Woolwich - BLs around C 65 9
Nottingham to Boston F 70 3
Nottingham to Kirkby Bentinck G 38 8
Nottingham to Lincoln F 43 7
Nottingham to Mansfield G 52 4
Nuneaton to Loughborough G 08 1

O
Ongar - Branch Line to E 05 5
Orpington to Tonbridge B 03 9
Oswestry - Branch Lines around E 60 4
Oswestry to Whitchurch E 81 9
Oxford to Bletchley D 57 9
Oxford to Moreton-in-Marsh D 15 9

P
Paddington to Ealing C 37 6
Paddington to Princes Risborough C819
Padstow - Branch Line to B 54 1
Peebles Loop G 19 7
Pembroke and Cardigan - BLs to F 29 1
Peterborough to Kings Lynn E 32 1
Peterborough to Lincoln F 89 5
Peterborough to Newark F 72 7
Plymouth - BLs around B 98 5
Plymouth to St. Austell C 63 5
Pontypool to Mountain Ash D 65 4
Pontypridd to Merthyr F 14 7
Pontypridd to Port Talbot E 86 4
Porthmadog 1954-94 - BLa B 31 2
Portmadoc 1923-46 - BLa B 13 8
Portsmouth to Southampton A 31 4
Portugal Narrow Gauge E 67 3
Potters Bar to Cambridge D 70 8
Preston to Blackpool G 16 6
Preston to Lancaster G 74 6
Princes Risborough - BL to D 05 0
Princes Risborough to Banbury C 85 7

R
Railways to Victory C 16 1
Reading to Basingstoke B 27 5
Reading to Didcot C 79 6
Reading to Guildford A 47 5
Redhill to Ashford A 73 4
Return to Blaenau 1970-82 C 64 2
Rhyl to Bangor F 15 4
Rhymney & New Tredegar Lines E 48 2
Rickmansworth to Aylesbury D 61 6
Romania & Bulgaria NG E 23 9
Ross-on-Wye - BLs around E 30 7
Ruabon to Barmouth E 84 0
Rugby to Birmingham E 37 6
Rugby to Loughborough F 12 3
Rugby to Stafford F 07 9
Rugeley to Stoke-on-Trent F 90 1
Ryde to Ventnor A 19 2

S
Salisbury to Westbury B 39 8
Salisbury to Yeovil B 06 0
Sardinia and Sicily Narrow Gauge F 50 5
Saxmundham to Yarmouth C 69 7
Saxony & Baltic Germany Revisited F 71 0
Saxony Narrow Gauge D 47 0
Scunthorpe to Doncaster G 34 0
Seaton & Sidmouth - BLs to A 95 6
Selsey - Branch Line to A 04 8
Sheerness - Branch Line to B 16 2
Sheffield towards Manchester G 18 0
Shenfield to Ipswich E 96 3
Shrewsbury - Branch Line to A 86 4
Shrewsbury to Chester E 70 3
Shrewsbury to Crewe F 48 2
Shrewsbury to Ludlow E 21 5
Shrewsbury to Newtown E 29 1
Sirhowy Valley Line E 12 3
Sittingbourne to Ramsgate A 90 1
Skegness & Mablethorpe - BL to F 84 0
Slough to Newbury C 56 7
South African Two-foot gauge E 51 2
Southampton to Bournemouth A 42 0
Southend & Southminster BLs E 76 5
Southern Alpine Narrow Gauge F 22
South London Line B 46 6
South Lynn to Norwich City F 03 1
Southwold - Branch Line to A 15 4
Spalding - Branch Lines around E 52
Spalding to Grimsby F 65 9 6
Stafford to Chester F 34 5
Stafford to Wellington F 59 8
St Albans to Bedford D 08 1
St. Austell to Penzance C 67 3
St. Boswell to Berwick F 44 4
Stourbridge to Wolverhampton E 16
St. Pancras to Barking D 68 5
St. Pancras to Folkestone E 88 8
St. Pancras to St. Albans C 78 9
Stratford to Cheshunt F 53 6
Stratford-u-Avon to Birmingham D 77
Stratford-u-Avon to Cheltenham C 25
Sudbury - Branch Lines to F 19 2
Surrey Narrow Gauge C 87 1
Sussex Narrow Gauge C 68 0
Swaffham - Branch Lines around F 9
Swanage to 1999 - BL to A 33 8
Swanley to Ashford B 45 9
Swansea - Branch Lines around F 38
Swansea to Carmarthen E 59 8
Swindon to Bristol C 96 3
Swindon to Gloucester D 46 3
Swindon to Newport D 30 2
Swiss Narrow Gauge C 94 9

T
Talyllyn 60 E 98 7
Tamworth to Derby F 76 5
Taunton to Barnstaple B 60 2
Taunton to Exeter C 82 6
Taunton to Minehead F 39 0
Tavistock to Plymouth B 88 6
Tenterden - Branch Line to A 21 5
Three Bridges to Brighton A 35 2
Tilbury Loop C 86 4
Tiverton - BLs around C 62 8
Tivetshall to Beccles D 41 8
Tonbridge to Hastings A 44 4
Torrington - Branch Lines to B 37 4
Tourist Railways of France G 04 3
Towcester - BLs around E 39 0
Tunbridge Wells BLs A 32 1

U
Upwell - Branch Line to B 64 0
Uttoxeter to Macclesfield G 05 0
Uttoxetor to Buxton G 33 3

V
Victoria to Bromley South A 98 7
Victoria to East Croydon A 40 6
Vivarais Revisited E 08 6

W
Walsall Routes F 45 1
Wantage - Branch Line to D 25 8
Wareham to Swanage 50 yrs D 09 8
Watercress Line G 75 3
Waterloo to Windsor A 54 3
Waterloo to Woking A 38 3
Watford to Leighton Buzzard D 45 6
Wellingborough to Leicester F 73 4
Welshpool to Llanfair E 49 9
Wenford Bridge to Fowey C 09 3
Wennington to Morecambe G 58 6
Westbury to Bath B 55 8
Westbury to Taunton C 76 5
West Cornwall Mineral Rlys D 48 7
West Croydon to Epsom B 08 4
West German Narrow Gauge D 93 7
West London - BLs of C 50 5
West London Line B 84 8
West Wiltshire - BLs of D 12 8
Weymouth - BLs A 65 9
Willesden Jn to Richmond B 71 8
Wimbledon to Beckenham C 58 1
Wimbledon to Epsom B 62 6
Wimborne - BLs around A 97 0
Wirksworth - Branch Lines to G 10 4
Wisbech - BLs around C 01 7
Witham & Kelvedon - BLs a E 82 6
Woking to Alton A 59 8
Woking to Portsmouth A 25 3
Woking to Southampton A 55 0
Wolverhampton to Shrewsbury E 44
Wolverhampton to Stafford F 79 6
Worcester to Birmingham D 97 5
Worcester to Hereford D 38 8
Worthing to Chichester A 06 2
Wrexham to New Brighton F 47 5
Wroxham - BLs around F 31 4

Y
Yeovil - 50 yrs change C 38 3
Yeovil to Dorchester A 76 5
Yeovil to Exeter A 91 8
York to Scarborough F 23 9